1996

WITH BRASS AND GAS

WITH
BRASS
AND GAS

An Illustrated and Embellished Chronicle of Ballooning in Mid-Nineteenth Century America

BY MUNSON BALDWIN

ILLUSTRATED BY
OWEN WOOD

BEACON PRESS
BOSTON

Permission is acknowledged to reprint passages from *Ballooning* by Charles H. Gibbs-Smith, published by Penguin Books, Ltd.; from *The Old Flying Days* by Charles C. Turner, published by S. Low, Marston & Co., Ltd. (Curtis Brown, Ltd.); and from *Jambo* by Anthony Smith, Copyright © 1963, published by E. P. Dutton & Co., Inc. (New York) and by George Allen and Unwin Ltd. (London) under the title *Throw Out Two Hands*.

NOTE

THIS is an unusual book. It is concerned with ballooning in the year 1859 and with the men who dedicated their lives to that pursuit; but, in a larger sense, it becomes a revealing comment about the United States and its people of that time.

The book is presented in almost scrapbook form. It consists entirely of excerpted and edited material from newspapers, magazines, books, letters, speeches, editorials, poetry, telegrams, headlines, announcements, and advertisements, as well as firsthand accounts by the balloonists (often called aeronauts) and the people who observed them.

To clarify the nature of these diverse items, different styles and faces of type have been used, along with varying lengths of lines and depths of columns. Facsimile reproduction has not been attempted, but the typography has been planned to impart the flavor of the period.

The artist has thoroughly researched the period in order to make his illustrations completely authentic within the context of this American era.

CONTENTS

Chapter 10

Chapter 11

Chapter 12

SOURCES

BOOKS

Coxwell, Henry T. *My Life and Balloon Experiences.* 2 vols. London: W. H. Allen & Co., 1887–89.

Gibbs-Smith, Charles H. *Ballooning.* London: Penguin Books, 1948.

Glaisher, James (ed.), et al. *Travels in the Air.* London: R. Bentley, 1871.

—————— (ed.). *The Atmosphere.* Translated from the French of Camille Flammarion. New York: Harper and Brothers, 1873.

Poole, John. *Crotchets in the Air. . . .* 2nd ed. London: H. Colburn, 1838.

Sala, George A. H. *The Life and Adventures of George Augustus Sala. . . .* New York: C. Scribner's Sons, 1895.

Smith, Anthony. *Jambo.* New York: The New American Library of World Literature, Inc., 1963.

Turner, Charles C. *The Old Flying Days.* London: S. Low, Marston & Co., Ltd., 1927.

Turnor, Christopher H. *Astra Castra.* London: Chapman & Hall, 1865.

Wise, John. *A System of Aeronautics. . . .* Philadelphia: J. A. Speel, 1850.

MAGAZINES

"Aerial Voyages," *British Quarterly Review,* LIV (London: Oct., 1871), 302–35.

"Balloonry," *The Knickerbocker,* LIV (New York: Oct., 1859), 380–84.

"Comets," *Fraser's Magazine,* LXV (London: Jan., 1862, 95–110.

Glaisher, James. "On Aerial Navigation . . .," *Good Words for 1863,* IV (London: 1863), 219–25.

Stedman, Edmund. "Aerial Navigation," *Scribner's Monthly*, XVII (New York: Feb., 1879), 566–81.

"The Babes in the Clouds," *All the Year Round*, XX (London: Sept., 1868), 347–49.

"Up in a Balloon," *Once a Week*, III (London: Aug., 1860), 178–80.

Verne, Jules. "A Voyage in a Balloon," *Sartain's Magazine*, X (Philadelphia: May, 1852), 389–95.

NEWSPAPERS

Adrian (Michigan) *Daily Watchtower; Evening Expositor;* 1858–59.

Atchison (Kansas) *Weekly Champion;* 1859.

Buffalo (New York) *Daily Courier;* 1859.

Cincinnati (Ohio) *Daily Enquirer; Gazette;* 1858–59.

Cleveland (Ohio) *Plain Dealer;* 1859.

Harper's Weekly (New York); 1858–59.

Illustrated London News; 1858.

Leavenworth (Kansas) *Herald of Freedom;* 1859.

Leslie's Illustrated Newspaper (New York); 1858–59.

New York *Evening Post; Express; Herald; Sun; Times; Tribune;* 1858-59.

Niagara Falls (New York) *Daily Gazette;* 1859.

North San Juan (California) *Hydraulic Press;* 1858.

Rochester (New York) *Union and Advertiser;* 1859.

St. Joseph (Missouri) *Weekly West;* 1859.

The Scientific American (New York); 1859.

MANUSCRIPTS

Barraclough, F. "Ballooning Lecture," delivered at Leeds, England, 1906.

WITH BRASS AND GAS

CHAPTER 1

Professors Bannister and Thurston,
two local aeronauts, are introduced
. . . All of the parts of a balloon are
shown and explained . . . Thurston,
the more professional of the two,
recalls a flight.

TODAY'S ADVERTISEMENTS

GRAND BALLOON ASCENSION!!

Prof. W. D. Bannister proposes to make one of his grand ascensions from the city of Adrian (the elements permitting), on Saturday, September 4th, in Prof. Ira J. Thurston's new and splendid Aerial Ship *Adrian!!!* This stupendous machine is constructed of the best India silk, is 126 feet in circumference, and holds the enormous amount of 240,000 gallons!

The inflation will commence at 8 A.M., and the ascension will take place as soon as a sufficient quantity of gas is received from the city gas works. It is the intention of Prof. Bannister to go but a few miles and return to the city with his balloon still inflated; and then to gratify any of his friends who wish to ascend a few hundred feet — a rope being attached — for which a small fee will be charged.

The ascension will doubtless be grand and we expect all the people from the rural districts to watch it.

Adrian, Michigan, August 28th

. . . a black speck, no bigger than a man's hand, was seen a little northwest of this city.

The speck grew larger and larger until, at last, the impression began to prevail that it was no less than our townsmen, Profs. Bannister and Thurston.

As they gradually approached—the balloon slowly increasing its dimensions—every man, woman, and child was out to watch its movements.

After having hung for nearly an hour in full view, they calmly and slowly descended a short distance southwest of the city where they were followed by crowds of horse and footmen . . .

* * *

Supposing all to be over, the curious spectators retired; when, about five o'clock, the whole town was again astir. Standing in the car, the huge globe above still distended, almost touching the sides of the houses, the aeronauts glided through the streets at a slight elevation from the ground, drawn, or rather guided, by a number of young men and boys who had attached themselves to the rope which led from their car. In this way, with hats in hand, and amid the cheers of their fellow-citizens, they proceeded to the Square . . .

A BALLOON is in essence a thin envelope (C) filled with a gas lighter than air. The envelope has three main openings: first the *valve* (A) in the crown, which can only be operated by the *valve line* (AA). This simply hangs down inside the envelope and out through the large second main opening or *neck* (N). The neck is left open throughout the flight so that when the balloon rises, the expanding gas can blow off harmlessly without bursting the envelope.

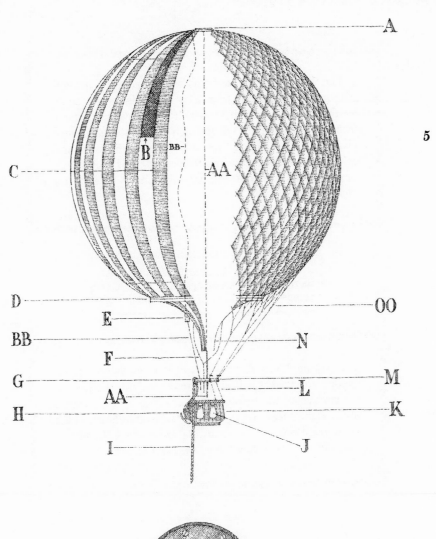

5

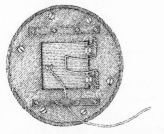

INSIDE VIEW OF THE VALVE

The third opening, used only when landing, is the *ripping panel* (B), made to pull away inside the envelope by the *ripping line* (BB) which is always kept away from its neighbor, is led through its own small *sleeve* (E), is dyed bright red to avoid tragic confusion, and coiled in a red bag attached to the *hoop* (M). With the ripping panel torn out, the balloon deflates in a matter of seconds.

After a rest of about fifteen minutes there, it soon became evident that another ascension was about to be attempted . . .

Covering the envelope is the *net,* whose function it is to support the basket and distribute the weight evenly over the surface of the balloon. The cording is first reduced to the *crow's feet* (OO), then to the leading lines which are toggled onto the hoop or ring, from which the basket (K) or "car" is suspended by the *car lines* (L).

Thurston

The scene here presented a mixture of excitement and confusion, making it impossible to do anything with system or order. No one understood my intentions when desiring them to hold on to the machine until I had it again properly graduated. Then a gentleman from the South was introduced to me, who commenced a conversation which drew away my attentions, and finally I received the heart-sickening information that the network was fast giving way about the top of the balloon—so large a rupture they said, that a bulb as big as a hogshead was protruding through it . . .

A small but important item is the *neck line* (F), which is attached to the bottom of the envelope. In flight it is tied to the hoop, and its main job is to hold down the bottom of the envelope when it is flabby through loss of gas, and so prevent the snarling of valve and ripping lines. In an emergency it is immediately cut and the envelope then floats up into the top of the net and forms a parachute.

Some cried, "send him up," with powerful efforts on their part to suit the action of the word, while others were equally determined to hold the car down. I roared at the top of my voice, "For God's sake, gentlemen, will you give me a chance to make the ascension?" But before I could even properly adjust my instruments or make the least calculation of the balloon's upward power, with a considerable projectile force we shot up through the air like a ball from a gun. The envelope expanded rapidly, the opening in the seam increased, and precipitatingly we began to sink, striking the top of a chimney and rebounding over a vacant lot in which we rudely descended.

An immense crowd again gathered, for it was only three squares from the place we first started.

So ended the experiments with my muslin balloon, a very inferior machine, cumbersome with repairs and recoatings, a machine that had given me much more trouble than reputation as a skillful aeronaut.

The *valve* should consist of one disk of Spanish cedar, placed outside the balloon at its top center, and another disk on the corresponding inside, and thus screwed together, clasping the silk. Then a hole four inches square is cut through the center, offering free communication for the gas to escape . . .

I had, though, procured a lot of silk with which to build a new one. Having now been at considerable expense, although the strictest economy had been observed, it was suggested that a public exhibition of the contemplated ascension, at fifty cents admission, would meet the expenditures of inflation . . .

The *clapper* overlaps the opening, with light brass hinges, or just as the mechanic fancies. A wire coil spring of the kind used in the common mousetrap, curves over and onto the clapper, making it self-shutting, since the pressure of the gas against it means nothing.

This announcement brought down upon me from friends all the forebodings that timid minds could predict on the anticipation of a balloon riot, because ascensions, from repeated failures in their attempts, and mobs, had become synonymous ideas with a great portion of the people who were attracted to them. However, I decided upon the plan of a publicly advertised ascension.

Another oddment is the *dripflap* (D), which leads rain and moisture off the balloon and clear of the crew.

Saturday turned out to be a blustry, stormy day. At 9 o'clock A.M., *the great silk bag was half lying, half sitting on the ground, being stuffed with gas from a 6-inch pipe and swelling visibly, like a very fat, drunken old lady, lolling her head about and making ineffectual efforts to get up . . .*

There are three gases used in ballooning: hydrogen is by far the lightest, but very inflammable; helium is best as it does not burn, but is very expensive; and coal gas is inflammable but much the cheapest, so, since its introduction for ballooning in 1821, the most commonly used . . .

Two hours later, there she was, but what a change! No longer the drunken old woman, but an upright, graceful, intelligent-looking creature, straining at her bands and longing to be off.

The main instruments and controls essential to the pilot are the valve line (kept coiled in a white bag attached to the hoop), the ripping line, the neck line, bags for ballast (generally 20 or 30 pounds each) (J), an altimeter (barometer) for height recording, and a statoscope for rate of fall or climb. Also a map and compass should be carried to enable the aeronaut to tell where he is going.

When the balloon is inflated, kept down by bags hooked onto the rigging, the basket is attached and the crew goes aboard. Ballast bags are then removed until the ground crew are able to hold her down easily by hand.

She is thus tried for lift, or "weighed off," and a further amount of ballast removed; 20 pounds is all right for a calm day, 50 pounds for a windy one . . .

The whole machine was restrained by two dangling cords, each held by two men. When I cut one cord it was to be the signal to let the other go.

I now watched for the moment when the balloon was rising in her vibrations caused by the gale . . .

. . . and at that moment I cut the cord . . .

It is therefore infinitely more safe to abandon the machine entirely to the air, because it then stands perfectly balanced and not at all fatigued.

. . . but the other men, instead of being punctual in letting theirs go, clung to it. The machine dragged them along with several more who seized hold of the rope, seeing its furious career, until they were all brought up against a high board fence where they all had to let go—just at the moment when the enormous bag was most depressed by the gale. With a tremendous swing, the car was dashed up against the eaves of the house, snapping the cords on the side of the basket which struck, letting down that side and spilling us out onto the roof, stunned.

Getting to our feet, we beheld the balloon plunging into a chasm of black, dense clouds. The expansive power of the gas, of course, burst it.

By this time, a gentleman in the house came to the window and offered assistance. . . .

In consequence of the high wind, a disaster occurred to Prof. Thurston's balloon on Saturday, which rendered it necessary to postpone the ascension. An immense number of people from far and near who came to see the flight were obliged to go home disappointed. Another day will soon be named and the ascension will be made as proposed, without fail.

*We shall soon see the atmosphere as full of balloons as are
the rivers and bays now of pleasure yachts.*

But its danger! exclaim a hundred voices.

*But my many ascensions under disadvantageous circum-
stances! is the reply. I can say that already half a dozen persons
have taken my balloons with no other knowledge than the simple
instructions given them on a sheet of paper, and have made ascensions as successful as myself. Some of these have since constructed their own balloons. . . .*

Also toggled onto the hoop are two stout ropes, of
which the most important is the *trail rope* (I). At low
altitude it trails on land or water and acts as an auto-
matic ballast. It is generally let down soon after takeoff.

As more rope is deposited on the ground, the balloon
is to that extent lightened and tends to rise again; as it
rises, it lifts more rope off the ground and so its ascent is
checked. In this fashion you can go for miles under favorable circumstances and in a light wind, the balloon
ever in advance of the trail rope, thus at all times by
means of the compass indicating the exact direction of
her course.

The appearance of a balloon in the sky
is always a signal for a certain amount of
commotion. Dogs begin to bark, poultry
run to and fro in evident dismay, while
cattle stand gazing up or scamper off in
terror.

On my first aerial voyage, we heard cries expressive of astonishment, fright, and anger; but the feeling of fright seemed to predominate. We distinctly saw women in their chemises look hurriedly out of windows and then rush back again. We saw chubby boys watching us, and blubbering as if they were mad. Some men, more determined than the rest, fired off guns at us. I saw several mammas, pointing us out to stubborn babies, with an attitude which seemed to say that our balloon was Old Bogey. Other women raised their hands against us, and at their signal many others ran away, making the sign of the cross. . . .

The attraction of ballooning, apart from the spectator's attitude toward showmanship, is the experience of smooth and silent flight, with superb sky and landscapes.

Rising above the earth, the traveler views its surface as a map stretched out on a boundless plain. Hillsides brown with the vine, furrows golden with grain, verdant meadows, cragged mountains whose tops are covered with somber forests, sparkling streams and sinuous rivers running to the distant ocean—all the charms, soft or stern, of landscapes and perspective, are slowly revealed to the delighted gaze of the aeronauts who, without feeling the slightest movement, hover as in a dream. . . .

Balloon flight, unless expertly directed, tends to be a series of ups and downs. This is due to the balloon's overshooting its theoretical equilibrium point on an up-run and becoming too heavy; whereupon it starts a down-run and gathers momentum until checked by throwing out ballast. The longer you wait to throw, the more you have to throw. The experienced pilot will do all he can to keep the height he desires by immediately correcting the down-run. Even a handful of sand is effective when near equilibrium.

In the old days, bits of paper or streamers were used instead of a statoscope to show if you were going up or down.

I could look up the balloon and see the meshes of the network showing through it, the upper valve and its springs and line, reaching to the car, and the geometrical form of the balloon itself.

For a time we remained almost stationary over a limekiln, bobbing up and down, and up again, in the hope of meeting with a current that would carry us somewhere. But up or down it was the same thing; there never was known a worse season for currents, so that at each descent, there was the eternal limekiln beneath us, and no one seemed inclined to make that the landing point. In vain also did our captain endeavor to elude the rabble (whose voices we distinctly heard) by hiding himself in the clouds. No sooner did we reappear than again their shouts would salute us . . .

I was stretching my head over the side of the car and contemplating the world of wonder below; listening to a dyspeptic gentleman immediately behind me who, as a preventative to extreme nervousness, had taken nothing but vegetables for dinner that day.

Then two of the passengers who had supplied themselves with an extraordinary stock of courage previous to starting, began quarreling. Could the pair have got to close quarters, the dispute would certainly have assumed a more serious character; for, jammed tight together as we were in the car, the least attempt at violence would certainly have ended in discharging the whole human cargo onto the railway station now below. But as it was, it did appear most ludicrous that two rational beings must choose that place for engaging in some paltry squabble . . .

No motion is experienced in flight, as the balloon goes at the same speed as the wind. The greatest windstorm is utterly powerless and inefficient in respect to its influence upon the balloon. The aeronaut might hold a lighted candle without extinguishing the flame. So long as the balloon is left free to pursue her own course upon the same level, this state of things remains uninterrupted.

The balloon is already approaching the earth. The trees, hedges, roads, and other features of the rural landscape, which for some time back have been growing gradually upon the eye, have resumed their original distinctness. Several persons also can now be distinguished, either standing in mute astonishment, looking up at our approach, or hurrying from all directions in the hope of being present at our descent.

A man on a black horse is in hot pursuit up the road—the horse's head and tail in a straight line. The race is beautiful and exciting. He is losing ground at every jump. Now he holds up a mile behind.

An amount of ballast was dropped, and so long was the heavy bag in getting to the ground that as the eye watched it fall and fall, the mind was filled with amazement at the height the balloon was still in the air. Suddenly the sound as of a gun announced that the bag had struck the soil. . . .

> For the perfect convenience and comfort of the parties, they must neither be brought to the earth with violence, jerked out of the car, hurled against buildings, nor run amongst trees; they must neither be landed in a quagmire, on the top of a house, in the rigging of a ship, nor decanted into a river . . .

The forests and parks, no longer an indefinite mass of something green, opened at our approach, separating into individual trees, leaves, and branches, appearing in quick succession, rapidly receding in our rear. At length, the field we have been so long aiming at appears directly before us . . .

The other rope fastened to the hoop above the basket ends in a *grappling hook* or anchor. For quick landing, the grappling hook can be dropped before ripping.

The soil must be of such a nature as will facilitate the attachment of the balloon; it must not be so hard that the hook cannot easily penetrate, nor so light that, having entered, it is unable to retain its hold . . .

The hook took hold in a branch of one of the trees, which broke off and dragged along. At this moment I perceived a countryman mounting the top rail of a worm fence about a hundred paces ahead of the balloon, to which point the wind was now driving it. We hailed him to assist. He looked in every direction but upward, and in another moment the limb and hook came square up against the panel of the fence upon which he was sitting, and threw it down, pitching the man head foremost onto the meadow before him, from which he sprung terrorstricken. He was soon out of sight. . . .

Last, though not least, some regard must be had for the tenants of the soil itself. Much care should therefore be taken to avoid attempting to descend in a place where the crops are of such a nature as to suffer from the operation, a practice extremely reprehensible, tending to bring disparagement upon the art, trouble to future aeronauts, and frequently much inconvenience to the parties themselves, which the possession of a little skill would have enabled them to avoid.

The hook then took effect in an orchard, which so alarmed a man who was plowing in the next field as to infect his horses, two boys, and two dogs near him, and to create a perfect bedlam amongst them. The horses ran away with the plow—snuffing the air like war steeds, the boys screamed, the dogs barked, the horses snorted and reared up in the fence corner. The man lay on his back looking up in terror, the balloon was surging up and down, ripping the grappling hook from one peach tree to another; and now the contagion had spread to the house and barnyard. The poultry were in a clatter; the matron of the domicile standing before the door of the house, clapping her hands together in anguish for the safety of the boys who were still screaming.

The old man next made his appearance with gun in hand, and in a gruff voice exclaimed, "Where is it, where is the d—— thing?" We made no delay in cutting in twain the grappling rope.

16

There are two ways of landing a balloon. If there is very little wind, you can valve right down and keep the valve open to deflate. If there is a fair wind blowing, it is best to valve down slowly to below 25 feet, and then rip . . .

Immediately after this, the bottom of the car struck the ground and the balloon pitched onto its side.

"For Heaven's sake, hold fast!" he shouted, as we all rolled in the car, one on the other, with each fresh lurch of the giant machine stretched on the ground before us, and from which we could hear the gas roaring like the blast of a furnace.

Again, we were pitched right on end, and the bottom of the car shifted into a ditch, the contents of which bubbled up through the wickerwork; and I who was stationed in that part to which the concussions were mostly confined, found myself sitting in a pool of water.

Then began a furious, disordered race. Trees, thickets, walls, all disappeared before us, broken or burst through by the shock.

"Sit tight, all of you, I say!" roared our pilot, as he saw some-one endeavoring to leave the car.

We plunged into a bog, the thick mud of which entered our mouths and eyes. It was maddening. "Stop! Stop!" they shouted, enraged with the monster which was dragging us. We were then carried along for half a mile until we reached a creek or small river through which we hurried, half buried in its waters, to the opposite bank, over which we bounded like a tennis ball. There appeared to be a general panic. We who sat down were trampled upon by the others. It was a scramble, each man for himself, the more powerful men thrusting back the weaker. Some of those climbing out first, abandoned their hold of the moving car as soon as it reached solid ground; others held on but were obliged to let go when the balloon, relieved of the weight of several persons, rose again with renewed buoyancy. A railway came before us—a train passing; it stopped at our cries, but we carried away the telegraphic posts and wires. . . .

Mere experience is by no means sufficient; for men may ascend for hundreds of times and still keep bungling on to the end. There must be a judgment to interpret its suggestions, and a coolness to apply them; penetration to embrace all that is requisite at a view and a quickness in calculating the results; prudence to avoid danger, and courage to confront it . . .

The wind blew hard now and it was dark. Our balloon drove on with prodigious rapidity. I could not see my compass, and we were not allowed to light a lucifer match under any pretext whatsoever. We descended to within 150 yards of the earth. Beneath us we saw a flat, marshy country of sinister aspect. Everyone listened with all his ears. There was no light whatever, and it became more and more difficult to guess where we were going.

"I am entirely out of my reckoning," he exclaimed, "and my opinion is that the only thing we have to do is to descend at once."

"What, here in the marshes?" remonstrated all of us.

The balloon went driving on still.

"We cannot descend here," the other aeronaut said, "we are over water."

Two or three of us looked over the edge of the car, and affirmed that we were not over water, but trees.

"It is water," he persisted.

Everyone now looked out attentively, and as the balloon descended a little, we saw plainly that there was no water.

At that moment the other aeronaut exclaimed, "I see a railway." It turned out that what he took for a railway was a canal which we had passed over a few minutes before. At this, the excitement got intense. Some prayed aloud, others shouted to "let off the gas"—in short, they behaved in the wildest manner, completely losing their self control. Several of the party pulled at the valve cord with great violence, tearing the valve door completely off its hinges and bringing it down into the car. Immediately afterwards we heard a noise similar to the escape of spare steam in a locomotive, and the lower part of the balloon collapsed rapidly. Mr. Gypson cried out, "Good Heavens! what has gone?" to which our captain answered, "The valve is gone! We are all dead men!" or words to that effect; and that same instant the balloon began to fall with appalling velocity; the immense mass of loose silk surging and rustling over our heads as it flapped to and fro between the network and cords.

Two of our party directly gave way to exclamations of extreme terror, in the midst of which the suggestion was made to throw everything over. I had two sandbags in my lap, which were

grabbed and cast away directly. We all began to hunt amongst our feet for whatever we could find, which was instantaneously thrown out; but no effect was perceptible. The wind still appeared to be rushing up past us at a fearful rate. . . .

> Standing orders for the crew at landing are to bend knees, grab the side of the basket or power lines (never the hoop), and stay in the basket until the deflation is advanced enough to make it possible for the lightened balloon to set off again. In the old ballooning days, perilous landings were common . . .

He was now having trouble with the ripping panel, and shouted that the rest of us must all jump clear together the moment the balloon struck. Accordingly, we knelt on the edge of the basket, legs outward, following his example. In a few moments the trail rope was in the trees tearing through them, setting up a continual jolting in the basket. We all hung outside, holding onto the rigging, and thus we crashed down through the trees to the sound of rending branches, striking the ground so heavily we all fell off. The balloon paused for a moment as if to take a breath, and then off it went, with a force a hundred men could not have stemmed; and I, who snatched at the trail rope just as it was gathering speed, was simply hurled aside like a mere twig, rolling over and over on the ground. I promptly let go.

Presently, some drab-smocked countrymen appeared. . . .

> Did you ever see the death of a balloon? Its grand and graceful form standing out in bold relief against the somber sky, already crippled by the expulsion of some quantity of its breath of life? It heaves and pants and groans till, its throes becoming fainter and fainter, it finally gives up the gas and lies stretched on the earth—as flat as a pancake! And *there's* a touch of the sublime for you.

There are two ways of dealing with aeronauts; the first is to invite them to dinner and offer them beds for the night; the other is to make an extortionate claim for damages and carry them before the magistrates as trespassers. The latter practice is much in vogue in rustic regions. You have scarcely leaped out of the car when up comes an angry farmer, vociferating loudly, gesticulating frantically; and when he sees his fences broken down, his crops trampled underfoot by a crowd of villagers who rush to inspect the stranger from the clouds, his wrath rises to the boiling point and he threatens immediate arrest, or appears to be on the eve of inflicting personal chastisement. . . .

* * *

The villagers would often proceed falteringly to the spot where the balloon lay, now heaving with strange contortions. At length, one of the crowd, more intrepid than the rest, stalks carefully to within shot, takes aim with his fowling piece and fires, tearing the balloon so severely that it begins to collapse rapidly. He gives a shout of triumph, whereupon the rest, summoning up courage, dart forward and bat it with flails or gash it with pitchforks. The outrush of gas is great, and causes a poisonous stench. Again, all retire; but when the dying monster appears exhausted, they tie the cause of alarm to a horse's tail, who gallops across the country, tearing it to shreds.

The air is the most delightful passageway between two localities. Nowhere is the path so buoyant, the climate so pure, the impediments so few. Cars and steamers would surely hide their heads and retreat to the home of the forgotten arts if they should once see a promenading balloon, large enough to carry a whole city in its folds, and so gentle as to obey every touch of its master. The swinging motion and the mountain scenery would be combined to give delight to locomotion . . .

If the aeronaut comes down on a forest in a strong wind, the car will rebound the moment it strikes the elastic branches of the tree tops, and the machine will thus ricochet along without any unpleasant consequences, and at the first clear space he can make his landing.

Have any commensurate efforts yet been made to achieve this result? Has it been considered otherwise than as a fantastic dream? Have any, save a few enthusiasts—mostly poor and unlearned—attempted to realize it? Visionary speculators waste fortunes upon impossible motors, luckless wells and mining shafts, while here is the most tempting of all material achievements demonstrably within the bounds of invention. The determined effort and liberal expenditure of government or of one of our moneyed corporations can solve the problem. It is strange that a score of such efforts, of such expenditures, are not making; that the deftest intellects are not devoted to the attainment of this end . . .

If the balloon happens to come down on a river or a lake, there is no cause for alarm, as the car will not sink many inches in the water. If it is calm weather, the car may be paddled along with very little effort.

Of all the productions of art, a balloon has thus far been the wildest and most untamable. A fantastic sprite, it has always been the fierce playfellow of the winds and clouds, and has refused to enter into aerial-like service; but the audacity of the present age threatens to subdue it. There is a new and sober determination growing up again in the way of its improvement.

A sufficiency of open, clean sward is desirable as this will favor the emptying and folding of the dismembered machine as soon as its task has been performed. The envelope or bag and equipment are packed into the basket for the homeward journey, followed by a round of toasts among aeronauts and crew, recounting the events of that afternoon.

Sights, oh! Such sights! Gulliver not fabulous. Men and women six inches tall; and as we rose, they diminished to five, four, three inches!

I am glad when I am down again, for I often imbibe a very contemptuous opinion of my species—a feeling common to many who are placed but the height of a mere carriage wheel above their fellow creatures . . .

24   *But what a lesson that short half hour would teach most men. Let them look down on some great city—even the largest and proudest in the world—now a poor, paltry Dutch toy of a town, having been placed on castors for the occasion, gently rolling away from beneath them—the greatest people of the earth, miserable little pigmies after all!*

SUNDAY SCHOOL CELEBRATION

and

BALLOON ASCENSION

ON THURSDAY, SEPTEMBER 16

PROF. W. D. BANNISTER

PROPOSES TO MAKE ONE OF HIS

GRAND ASCENSIONS

in the city of ADRIAN (the elements permitting)

IN IRA J. THURSTON'S NEW AND SPLENDID

AERIAL SHIP *ADRIAN*

Messrs. Bannister and Thurston have been instrumental in putting hundreds of dollars into the hands of businessmen of this city, and it will be a shame if they are allowed to suffer pecuniarily by making ascensions here. About half enough has been subscribed to pay them, and we hope that the honor of our city will be sustained by liberal contributions when the people are called upon tomorrow. . . .

GRAND ASCENSION BALL:

AT CITY HALL, FOR THE BENEFIT OF

PROF. W. D. BANNISTER

On Thursday Evening

CHAPTER 2

Professor Bannister tells of his flight with Thurston and of the terrible circumstances under which Thurston was last seen . . . Why were two balloons sighted? . . . What about Thurston and what of those children?

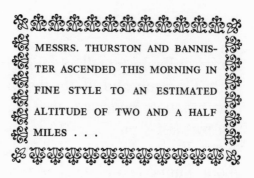

MESSRS. THURSTON AND BANNIS-
TER ASCENDED THIS MORNING IN
FINE STYLE TO AN ESTIMATED
ALTITUDE OF TWO AND A HALF
MILES . . .

> The auspicious day arrived. The country people, no ways daunted from the last failures, poured into town in a continuous stream, gathering around the large open common on its outskirts . . .

Bannister   *The windows and roofs of surrounding houses, scaffoldings of various form and contrivances, are crowded, forming to me a very interesting spectacle. They have viewed for hours, with fixed and silent attentions, the bustle around the apparatus and the gradual expansion of the balloon.*

I shook hands with my friends (who somewhat disturbed my nerve by unnecessarily taking an affectionate farewell of me), and walked in as unconcerned a manner as I could to the car. Indeed, the whole company viewed us with a kind of regret, as devoted persons whose return was at least problematical. As the eyes of the world were upon me, I climbed in. My dignity was slightly impaired by my hat's being knocked off by the hoop above the car. Upon this my friend was seated, tying up the opening with his pocket handkerchief.

I remember wagging my hand in a gentle way toward the crowd.

The words, "Let go," were given, and off we went . . .

> The first second or two of the balloon's ascent caused a stillness in the mass of people that seemed as though they were fixed immovably to the spot, when all of a sudden the very air began to reverberate with the shouts that followed . . .

I could detect no movements on the part of the balloon; the earth seemed to sink away rapidly from under our feet while we remained stationary. In a moment the Common appeared but a small patch beneath and behind us, and by the time I had recovered my nerve sufficiently to look about, we were some thousand feet above the world.

30

"The balloon—see the balloon!" At about the hour of noon these words were issuing from the mouth of every little urchin in the streets, which caused older heads to cast their eyes upwards in order to discover the cause, which was soon caught sight of in the rapid movement of a balloon. When last seen it was but a tiny sphere, a mere bubble in the sky, pursuing its noiseless way, as if it had escaped forever from this turbulent earth.

In a balloon you are entirely detached from the earth; there are no intermediate points by which the eye can be gradually conducted downwards; so that the impression of height upon the senses—which causes dizziness—is indefinite, vague. From the parapet of a house, or from a column, or a tall cliff, the eye is led by an intervening medium down to the base and dizziness ensues. Not so, however, from a balloon at any height.

The day was clear and pleasant, the atmosphere free from mist and smoke, and no objects intervened to shut out the variegated cities and country beneath.

The whole end of Lake Erie was studded with picturesque islands, an occasional vessel the only sign of life on the vast expanse of water. Nearer, was the city of Monroe buried in a rich grove, which only afforded an occasional sight of the buildings. Further to the south, lay Toledo and Maumee City; just underneath and behind was the city of Adrian, and the neighboring towns of Manchester, Tecumseh, and Quinton. The Michigan Southern Railroad and its branches were distinctly traced out, and the trains could be seen traveling along them. Still following around, the eyes rested on Detroit, its tall spires and endless mass of building, and the beautiful river which flows so silently by it. Farmers working in the field; characters moving along the highways; boats sailing upon the waters; the bustle and stir of city life, with the quiet and retirement of the country and prairies, rivers and lakes. . .

Blissfield, Mich.

The balloon was seen at ten minutes past twelve, in a northeast direction from this place and at that time not larger than a star in appearance.

In about forty minutes after they started, a telegraph dispatch was received from Toledo, stating that the balloon was in sight and apparently descending in the vicinity of Sylvania.

P.S. Since the above was in type, Mr. Bannister has arrived in the city and informs us that they descended near Knight's Station, that a number of men assisted them to land and secure the balloon, that they remained in the car about thirty minutes during which time the gas was escaping with slow progress from the valve. Thurston proposed to detach the car and turn the balloon down, so that he could reach the valve and let the gas escape from the mouth of the balloon. This was done while the men were holding fast to the balloon by the cordage which was being removed. Mr. Bannister says the mouth of the balloon was open and the gas was seen escaping.

Mr. Thurston climbed to the top end, where the valve is, and obtained a firm hold of the silk, compressed it, and seated himself astride the valve block, about thirteen inches in diameter, circular in shape, and of one-inch board. Thus seated, with his arms around the compressed silk, he told the others to let go and let up the mouth of the balloon. With its diameter of eighteen inches it was supposed it would quickly discharge the gas.

According to Mr. Thurston's order, the lower part of the balloon *was* thrown up. Mr. Thurston called out to Bannister, that "it would be all right." In an instant the whole jumped into the air carrying Mr. Thurston and his assistant with it, a Mr. Westerman, who fortunately was able to let go from not too great a height.

And that was the last which has been heard from Mr. Thurston, except that he was watched by Mr. Bannister and others for an hour, when he passed out of sight, a lost speck in the sky.

Mr. Bannister arrived on the 1 o'clock train, bringing the basket and netting of the balloon and the sad news. He watched the balloon with a glass until it reached its highest elevation, and says that Thurston maintained his seat and seemed to be perfectly easy. . . .

It appears that it was customary with Mr. Thurston, when he had landed with his balloon, to bring the top to the ground and let the mouth turn up to hasten the escape of gas, in which position he would purposely let it carry him up and as the gas escaped rapidly, he would of course, come down after going a few rods. We have reason to believe that it was his intention to do so on this occasion. He said to the people who were present, that they need not be surprised if they should see another ascension immediately.

34

Col. Dan Munger, conductor on the Great Western (Canada) R. R. says that Prof. Thurston landed safely on Friday morning 16 miles from Baptiste Creek and was at Belle River yesterday.

Balch, Operator
Detroit

> The operator at Belle River says a balloon came down near there on Friday morning and went up again; didn't say if anyone landed or not.

It is positively asserted that a balloon has been found near Baptiste Creek. I am inclined to think that Munger's information is not well founded as regards Thurston.

Balch, Operator Detroit

The old lady said the people had seen a balloon as it passed up the lakeshore on Thursday: several times sailing out over the lake with the varying currents of air. Its elevation was different at various times, the balloon rising until it was as small as a man's hat and again descending to within a few feet of the trees. They distinctly saw Mr. Thurston clinging to it, a handkerchief tied around his head, and as he passed he drew up his feet several times and let them down as though they were tired or cramped. All united in the statement that he was hanging to the balloon, although they saw nothing strange in the perilous position he maintained, from ignorance of the manner of conducting such matters.

They stated that it passed on about eight or ten miles, until it lowered at the mouth of Baptiste Creek. . . .

To H. Hart—It is now uncertain as to Thurston's safety. The balloon landed near Baptiste Creek. Shall hear more at three o'clock.

Daniel Munger

36

Thurston

At length, I saw several men to whom I shouted for help. They, however, staring with vacant gaze, stood motionless like so many statues. I saw another batch of men to whom I made the same appeal, but with similar result. Some remained motionless; a man and a woman ran away at full speed and one tall fellow actually dropped on his face.

The thought had struck me several times to try, by any means, to make a rent in the balloon, for although I had no knife I might have torn the silk with my teeth.

But then it occurred to me that as soon as the gas escaped I should not be able to support the concussion. . . .

I was gradually coming near to the earth. I saw some men working in a field and shouted to them, "For God's sake, help me, or I shall be lost!"

They understood my appeal at last, but too late.

Coming to a farm, I shouted out the same appeal to the people standing there. Some women, with their quick, humane instinct, were the first to perceive my danger, and exhorted the men to hurry to my assistance, they themselves running as fast as they could, . . . but on I went.

I was now carried in a straight direction toward the lake which was but a short distance ahead.

* * *

Almost certain death seemed before me; yet to jump on this passage would have assured my being dashed to pieces on the ground beneath . . .

Six o'clock and moving over a thick wood.

My strength now almost forsook me; my lips were parched with thirst. . . .

Weight of the unfortunate man too great for the size of the valve.

The silk gave way.

Balloon valve on which Thurston sat, torn from the silk three-quarters of the way round.

His only remaining chance to cling to the smooth material. . . .

* * *

A boy, about twelve years of age, was attracted by a peculiar whistling noise as if some large bird was passing over, and looked up in time to see something fall in that piece of woods. . . .

He thought it must have been a paper balloon and started after it. . . .

He returned to the house and tried to get an elder brother to go with him after the paper balloon. He was laughed at for wanting to go so far after a bit of paper and finally gave it up. . . .

* * *

. . . and changing its course, sailed out over the lake as far as the lighthouse, and from thence inland several miles until it finally dropped . . . having been in the air about four hours. . . .

* * *

A Chicago paper which reached the city yesterday had a dispatch which states that two children were accidentally carried off in a balloon the evening of the seventeenth from Rome, eighteen miles east of Centralia.

This intelligence opened again the discussion in regard to the balloon (it is said there were two), which was the subject of so many conjectures.

On the evening of the 18th, one passed northeast, the other passed in the west over the entire length of the city.

A little later a large balloon was seen about sundown, passing at a considerable height northeast, toward Adrian. There are, besides, persons who saw both balloons at the same time.

Mr. J. A. Foster, the artist, informs us that while riding in his buggy soon after sundown they saw the balloon coming from the west, that it had perhaps run away from Centralia.

The lateness of the hour precluded any possibility of a critical examination of it, and by the time spy glasses were procured, it had disappeared.

Was it possible that the balloon seen here on Saturday evening was the one that carried off the children from Rome on the previous evening? If it was, what had become of the precious freight? the little ones whose loss had perhaps filled the hearts of the parents with grief that will follow them to the grave. If this was the balloon in which a father's passion for aerial navigation induced him to give his pets the pleasure of a ride in the air, they must have been lost before it reached here; for it is said by all who saw this, that nothing except the balloon and some dangling cords were perceptible. . . .

CHAPTER 3

*Events high in the heavens seem
to portend dire happenings nearer
earth . . . Thurston is still missing,
but the children are safe . . . A
reader recounts many tragedies.*

The papers all, both great and small, from
   Los Angeles to Yreka,
All tell a tale about the trail of the long-tailed heaven streaker.

But you might as well say, "The sun rose yesterday," and
   That the earth is a long way from it,
As to write long leaders, just to tell your seeing readers,
   That of evenings they can look upon the comet.

The whole world just now is more or less excited about comets, and comets, therefore, are a proper subject for journalistic reflections. Donati's comet is in full view and is attracting the attention of savants, professional and amateur, in both hemispheres.

Although the present comet is a mere dwarf compared with others

(its tail measuring only fifteen millions of miles in length), it has caused some sensation as being one of the few which has been visible to the naked eye. Everyone is acquainted with its appearance in the northwestern heavens during the evening when it may easily be recognized by its hazy aspect, and a tail pointed almost directly to the Pole Star. The best time to see it is early in the morning between three and four o'clock.

Comets consist for the most part of a large and more or less splendid but ill-defined nebulous mass of light called a head, which is usually much brighter towards its center, and offers the appearance of a vivid star or planet. From the head appear to diverge two streams of light which grow broader and more diffused, producing an effect like that of the trails left by some meteors or like the diverging fire of a skyrocket (only without sparks or perceptible motion).

We could tell of twinkling heads and undulating tails, and sparkling nuclei, and a bleak comae, and startling alternations of light, and dark vacancies. . . .

꙳

On the morning of October 1st at 5 A.M., the nucleus was very bright and also the beautiful circle of light that surrounded it. This brush-like circle somewhat resembled the tail of a peacock when spread open. The light of the brush appeared steady, but that of the tail very much represented the motions of fine particles of dust as seen in a darkened room when the sun is shining upon them.

Donati's comet varies materially from night to night. Its diameter, 1,560 miles on October 2nd; on the 5th, only 400 miles; the next night it was double that size.

Its distance from us about 52 millions of miles. . . .

Such a sight might not happen again during the very limited lifetime that is allotted to this degenerate people. A brilliant nucleus, the tail prodigious . . .

Its end shadowy, faint, tremulous, and uncertain. . . .

The condensed profusion of its beautiful white plume, as it stood right up night after night, in the dark autumnal sky. . . .

> It would seem that this comet has some occult, maddening influence on balloons. . . .

No trace of Thurston has been discovered, although the country has been thoroughly searched for him or his remains. The fact that the valve on which he sat appears to have been half torn off by his weight, lends color to the belief that he must have fallen off when his hands grew cramped with continuous holding on.

* * *

The office was crowded at seven o'clock in the morning, and in self defense, the balloon was taken out and suspended in front.

The balloon itself is a great curiosity, being upwards of sixty-five feet in length and fifty in breadth, when not inflated. It was secured in the middle and hung from the fourth story, both ends reaching nearly to the ground.

The street was soon occupied by a crowd, which came and went during the whole forenoon, gazing upon the balloon, examining its texture, and handling the small circular piece of board which constituted the aeronaut's seat. The opinions expressed were numerous. Some of them were ridiculous, but all managed to gain an understanding of the matter and went away satisfied.

In the afternoon, after the balloon had been taken down and stored away, troops of little children came marching from the various schoolhouses, anxious for a sight. They were accommodated and were much more demonstrative than the older visitors. . . .

In the same week, another involuntary ascent took place in which two children were carried, alone, into the air, but with a result which happily was of a different nature.

Mr. Wilson affected a beautiful ascent from the fairgrounds at Centralia, Iowa, on Friday the 17th, and descended twenty miles southeastward. He was caught by a tree about forty-five rods from the farmhouse of Mr. Benjamin Harvey. They pulled the car to the ground, the balloon was "towed" to the house, and Mr. Harvey prepared to have some sport by rising the length of the rope, to be pulled down. Proving too heavy to rise, he stepped out and put his three children in—a boy of three years, and a girl of eight, and a still older girl. Mr. Wilson called out to those holding the ropes to be sure to hold fast. The three children were too heavy and the eldest was taken out.

At this instance, through the unwatchfulness of the persons at the cords, the balloon suddenly and very swiftly went up. The anchor struck in a rail fence, but tore it away while a cry of horror burst from the group. The children screamed, and the pitiful appeal, "Pull me down, Father!" as it instantly grew fainter and fainter, rendered the parents, and indeed, all present at the time, perfectly frantic. It was now past seven o'clock, becoming dark, and the balloon was soon lost sight of.

As there was little wind, the balloon had gone almost directly upward, until its disappearance on the southeasterly course. Messengers were dispatched in every direction, and the alarm spread rapidly, creating everywhere the intensest excitement. In all quarters men and boys rallied in parties to scour the country and search the woods, in expectation that the victims would somewhere descend and be subjected to the perils of drowning, or else of starving undiscovered. The idea became current that they might encounter frigid atmospheres which they could not survive.

* * *

It was about three o'clock on Saturday morning when Mr. Ignatio Atchison got up and went out upon his porch "to see the blazing star"—the comet. An immense specter, rising from a tree about twenty yards distant, rather appalled him, and he re-entered his house. On coming out again, a weak and piteous voice called to him from the specter. "Come here and let us down; we are almost frozen!" Mr. Atchison mustered help, cut away several limbs of the tree, and drew the car in safety to the ground.

The little boy was first lifted out, and when placed upon his feet, instantly ran for several yards, then turned and for a moment contemplated the balloon with intense curiosity. The little girl told her sorrows and adventures to these people, who strangely indeed, had not heard of the disaster.

She said she passed over a town where she saw a great many people to whom she appealed at the top of her voice. This place was Centralia. The balloon was seen to pass over, but the people never imagined that it carried two persons in such danger.

When the sunlight all went away and the great comet came blazing out, little Johnny was apprehensive that the comet might come too near their airy craft, and set it on fire with a swish of its dreadful tail. But when his sister assured him that the fiery dragon was "as much as twenty miles away," and that God wouldn't let it hurt them, he was tranquilized, but soon afterwards said, "I wish it would come a little nearer, so I could warm myself—I'm so cold!"

Jenny took off her apron and wrapped it about the child, saying tenderly: "This is all your sister has to make you warm, darling, but she'll hug you close in her arms, and we will say our prayers and you shall go to sleep."

"How can I say my prayers, before I have my supper?" asked little Johnny.

"Sister hasn't any supper for you, or for herself, but we must pray all the harder," solemnly responded Jenny.

So the two wanderers, alone in the wide heavens, unawed by darkness, immensity, and silence, by the presence of the great comet and the millions of unpitying stars, lifted their little clasped hands and sobbed out their sorrowful prayer. Soon the younger, sitting on the bottom of the car, with his head leaning against his sister's knee, slept as soundly as though he were lying in his own bed at home, while the elder watched quietly through the long, long hours; and the car floated gently on in the still night air until it began to sway and rock on the fresh morning wind.

Who can divine that simple little child's thoughts, speculations, and wild imaginings, while watching throughout those hours? She may have feared coming in collision with a meteor—for many were abroad that night, scouts and heralds of the great comet—or perhaps being cast away on some desolate star island, or, more dreary still, floating and floating on, night and day, until they should both die of cold and hunger.

In handling the ropes, she happened to pull one which had the effect of bringing the balloon down. . . .

* * *

The youthful aerials were in the balloon about thirteen hours. Mr. Brooks, the aeronaut, concluded that they must have ascended at least four and one half miles before commencing to come down.

The happy result was received in Centralia and announced on Sunday morning in the churches. The children were brought there on Monday and welcomed with the firing of cannons.

Monroe, September 23rd:

Reports say that there is a person found in the marsh, fourteen or fifteen miles from this place. The supposition is that the body must be that of Mr. Thurston. Some persons will go from here in the morning for the place. It is hoped that some persons from Adrian who can identify him will come on the morning train.

— Telegraph operator, Monroe

There can be but little doubt of the identity of the body; and three of our citizens started from Monroe this morning to identify and bring home the remains if it is Mr. Thurston. We may have further news before going to press. The locality is four miles south of Huron. The body is said to be nearly buried in the earth.

September 25th =
    Monroe office says that body found near Huron is not that of Mr. Thurston. It has been in the water for some weeks.
            Cole, operator

We found the body, and we were very soon convinced that it could not be that of Mr. Thurston. These remains, very much decayed, were resting in the edge of the marsh, in about two feet of water, on the back side of a drift-log. The sediment was deposited on the body so that we could only distinguish that it was covered with some kind of clothing, completely rotten. From the collection of gas or air in a well-worn boot, one leg was drawn upward and the sole of the boot was near the surface of the water. One of our party took hold of the heel of the boot, and with a very slight pull, the leg disjointed at the knee. . . .

The boot and leg were dropped back to its place and we turned homeward without further disturbing the remains of the poor fellow, whose only monument is the tall grass waving in the lake breezes, and whose only funeral dirge has been the scream of the wild fowl and surging of the waters.

PROVIDENCE, RHODE ISLAND: The recent unfortunate and probably fatal balloon ascension of Mr. Thurston, which has created such a painful interest throughout the country, has also brought about, through the columns of the newspaper press, many scraps of history connected with balloon traveling. We have compiled a list of fatalities and do not know of one distinguished aeronaut who has not met with a violent death by means of the balloon. M. Pilatre and M. Romain of France made an ascent from Bologne, 1785, with a Montgolfier balloon, fire being kindled underneath, and the balloon ascended by means of rarefied air. At an amazing height, the balloon took fire, burned the cords by which the car was suspended, and the unhappy occupants were precipitated to the earth, dashing them to pieces. . . .

M. Zambecarri, accompanied by a friend, made an ascent from the same place, 1812. On his descent, the balloon became entangled in the branches of a high tree and caught fire. The aeronauts leaped out. Zambecarri was killed on the spot and M. Bugona survived but a short time. About the same time a mechanic named Brytore ascended from Mannheim. At a considerable height, he perceived too late that the vehicle was damaged. He opened the valve, descended with great velocity, and was dashed to pieces against a house.

Madame Blanchard ascended from Tivoli, 1819. At the height of four hundred feet her balloon caught fire. . . .

I saw her! She ascended in a balloon of small size, to save the expensive filling; she was therefore advised to inflate it entirely, and the gas escaped by the lower orifice leaving on its route a trail of hydrogen. Suspended above her car by an iron wire she carried a kind of framework, forming an aureola, which she was to kindle. She had often repeated this experiment. On this occasion she also carried a little parachute ballasted by a firework terminating in a ball with silver rain. She was to launch this apparatus after having lighted it.

She ascended. The night was dark. At the moment of lighting the firework, she was so imprudent as to let the lance pass beneath the column of hydrogen, which was escaping from the balloon. My eyes were fixed on her. Suddenly an unexpected flash illuminated the darkness. I thought it a surprise of the skillful aeronaut. This flame increased, suddenly disappeared, and reappeared at the top of the balloon in the form of an immense jet of burning gas. This sinister light projected over the Boulevard Momartre. Then I saw the unfortunate woman rise, twice attempt to compress the orifice of the balloon, to extinguish the fire, then seat herself in the car to seek to direct its descent. The combustion of the gas lasted for several minutes. The balloon, diminished by degrees, continue to descend, but this was not a fall! The balloon car alighted on the roof of a house. Shock was slight. "Help!" cried the unfortunate woman. I arrived in the street at that moment. The car slid along the roof, and then encountered an iron hook. At this shock, Madame Blanchard was thrown out of the car and precipitated onto the pavement! She was killed.

Mr. Harris was killed May 24, 1824. He went up from City Road, London; at the height of two miles he started to descend rapidly and was dashed to pieces.

Mr. Green ascended from Cardiff, 1849. His body was found some time after on the Capital Flat-house shoals, in the center of Bristol Channel.

M. Arran, a celebrated French aeronaut, ascended from Barcelona, in September, 1848. Nothing was heard of him until the middle of November, when his body was found near Rosas.

Lieutenant Gale ascended from the Hippodrome of Vincennes, September 8, 1850. Some days subsequently, the body was found in a clump of ferns, his limbs broken and mutilated, the face completely eaten away by dogs and other animals. . . .

He had been, I think, a lieutenant in the Royal Navy, but he had passed a good many years of his life in the United States, following what vocation I know not, but failing apparently to realize any substantial profits therefrom. He was a man of the most dauntless courage, and his early training as a seaman had given him that quickness of action, clearness of head, and readiness of resource, which are absolutely indispensable in what I may call a skipper of an aerial ship. He was a dreamer of dreams. He had no literary faculties; but he communicated his views to me, and I wrote a lecture for him on ballooning in general, which he was to deliver in a certain large and provincial town, allowing to me a handsome portion of the profits.

At this period, all England was talking about the vanished Arctic Expedition. The lieutenant had conceived the odd notion that the ships of the Expedition might be lying behind some gigantic icebergs; and his proposal was to proceed in a steamer specially fitted up for the purpose, to the Arctic regions, and make restricted or "captive" balloon ascents, in the hope of surveying vast tracts of icy deserts, and possibly alighting on some vestiges of the lost ships. I drew out for him a memorial to the Lords of the Admiralty, on which document I need scarcely say a plentiful *douche* of official cold water was properly poured. Then Gale bombarded the press with details of his scheme. A few of the newspapers inserted his communication; but this led to no greater result than a caricature and half a column in *Punch*.

The Lieutenant was miserably poor; he had a huge family of young children, and was wholly incompetent to put his views, or make interest in influential quarters. He centered his hopes on this itinerant lecture, illustrated by models and diagrams.

I took a week's holiday to see my friend, the Lieutenant, well started on his lecturing tour. At Hall, we engaged some assembly rooms for three nights. We had money enough to advertise the lecture pretty liberally in the local newspapers, which obliged us with a number of highly complimentary paragraphs, predicting brilliant success for the gallant Lieutenant Gale, R.N., the undaunted aeronaut and potential savior of the Expedition.

Alas! for the vanity of human wishes, and the fallacy of human hopes. The night came and I was the money-taker at the Assembly Rooms. Anxiously did I listen for the sound of footsteps ascending the stairs; but I am afraid, in the whole body of the hall and the gallery all around, our audience did not muster more than twenty-six, including half a dozen fisher-lads, who paid half price, and the inevitable old lady with the crushed bonnet and the big umbrella whom I have rarely known to be absent from the first night of any lecture in the civilized world.

The worst of it was, that sitting in my money-taker's box with nothing to do, I could hear the sonorous voice of Lieutenant Gale echoing through the almost empty hall, and interrupted at no infrequent intervals by cries of, "Shut up!", "Put your head in a bag!", and so forth.

The remaining two lectures were not delivered. As for the share which I was to have in the balloon, which I saw made, it was not productive, since, before the machine was complete, Lieutenant Gale accepted an engagement to make a series of ascents in Paris and other towns. At first, he was very successful, but a few weeks afterwards, he fell out of the car.

* * *

James Goulston made an ascent in the evening from The Bellevue Gardens, June 2, 1852. It being cloudy at the time, the car was lost from view in two minutes. He fell from his vehicle attempting to descend, at the town of Leeds; a considerable quantity of blood and brains, spattered over all, marked the spot where he struck the earth.

Mr. Knight ascended from Bombay, December 14, 1853, in the presence of a large concourse of natives, amongst whom was the Rajah of Dar who promised the aeronaut 200 rupees if he went up and came down again. The balloon went straight out to sea, and Mr. Knight has not been heard from since.

In September 1851, M. Merle was carried off by a balloon which broke from its moorings. Merle ascended to such a height that he was frozen to death. . . .

Mr. Timothy Winchester made an ascent from Norwalk, Ohio, in August, 1855. Starting in good spirits and amid the cheers of a large concourse of people, *he* has not been heard from since. He may have gone on an excursion to the North Star, as the last seen of him, he was passing rapidly over Lake Erie.

M. Godard, the distinguished French aeronaut, called upon us this morning. He is now on his way to Cincinnati, where he will meet Steiner, the great German aeronaut. Godard has challenged Steiner for a race in the air; Steiner has accepted, and each one is getting his best balloon in good flying trim.

Sporting circles are elated at the prospect of rare fun in the clouds.

A committee of five well-known citizens have been chosen, who were to act as judges, etc. They will decide if the weather in the morning shall justify the inflation of the balloons. When the inflation has commenced, the aeronauts must go.

The success of either will be in relation to distance, not height. Arrangements will be made for each aeronaut to send down at every town passed—in a parachute—a "log" or note, containing the name of the balloon which passes, and any incident occurring on the trip, which will then be sent by telegraph. Monsieur Godard and Professor Steiner each expect to be up three or four days.

The inflation of the balloons, each containing thirty-six thousand cubic feet of gas, will commence at 9 A.M., and the ascension will take place at 4 A.M. precisely.

Side betting will be animated without doubt. A race of this kind is something new under the sun.

Regarding our dear friend Thurston, I have thought of nothing, spoken of nothing I might almost say, for ten days past, but his awful departure. Knowing his indomitable perseverance, his undaunted courage and his never-failing hopefulness, I have waited confidently for the arrival by mail or telegraph, of the announcement of his safety. I have hoped on, from day to day, until consciousness has forced upon me the fact that he is gone from us forever. Only those who enjoyed the benefit of his friendship can appreciate the loss that we have all sustained.

But I commenced writing, not with the intention of penning a eulogy upon my departed friend, but to give you my idea of the cause of the catastrophe. For these views I am indebted to Professor John H. Steiner, the aeronaut who is about racing from Cincinnati, with M. Godard.

He tells me that when a balloon starts with an ascending power of even fifty pounds, it will run to an immense height *with the valve open* before it will part with an appreciable quantity of gas, because the speed with which the balloon rises is as great as that of the escaping gas; besides which, atmospheric resistance tends to retain the gas within the balloon. But there was another cause for Mr. Thurston's balloon's not parting with its gas sooner. The neck (which was upwards) was so long that it lay over on the side of the balloon a few inches, Mr. Westerman says, like the tied mouth of a full bag of grain . . .

Mr. J. Westerman also had hold of it at the time, and was lifted up about ten feet, when he let go, and fell to the ground. Mr. Westerman says that the mouth of the balloon was open, and he saw Mr. Thurston open it to the extent of eighteen inches. He noticed the cord by which the valve was operated passing through the opening, the end hanging outside. Mr. W. thinks that when the mouth of the balloon turned up and it arose in the air, this cord got entangled around the opening, and as the balloon stretched out with Mr. Thurston's weight, the cord being fast to the valve on the inside, was drawn down so as to entirely close the mouth, now at the top.

The fact, which was observed by Mr. Westerman's wife and daughter as well as others, that the mouth, with a portion of the collapsed balloon, like a neck, was lying on the distended portion, as the top of a great bag partially filled when tied would fall over upon the side, confirms these suspicions.

Professor Steiner says the *atmospheric pressure,* caused by the fearful speed of the rushing balloon, flattened it down and added to the difficulty of the gas escaping. The balloon continued ascending until the expansion, caused by the rarefied atmosphere in which it floated, and the cessation of speed from the same cause, allowed the gas to commence escaping and the balloon began its descent.

This explanation, it appears to me, is the true one.

I hope, ere this reaches you, to be informed of the recovery of our lamented friend's body; that the poor boon of granting him a decent burial may not be withheld.

Yours in sorrow,
C. H. H.

We have received a communication which was written under the impression that the body of the man found at Huron received no attention after it was ascertained that it was not Mr. Thurston. The fact is, as we were informed at the time, that the authorities of Monroe County were taking measures to have an inquest when the gentleman from this city left Monroe. This should have been mentioned at the time, to save the gentleman who saw the body from suspecting any unfeeling disregard of the "usual duties of citizens in a Christian land to bury the dead." Doubtless the inquest was held and the remains had a decent burial under the direction of the authorities of Monroe County, though we have not received any authentic account of what was done. . . .

CHAPTER 4

*Plans for a transcontinental trip
. . . The planners, Messrs. Wise,
La Mountain, and Gager, appear
to be a testy trio . . . Hot-air paper
balloons have their drawbacks.*

ST. LOUIS: Some time ago, we published an article relative to one of the grandest experiments ever projected in this country, viz.: a voyage through the air from St. Louis to a point on the Atlantic Coast, one thousand miles distant. However chimerical or hazardous this undertaking may be viewed, the attempt will assuredly be made. Prof. John Wise, the well-known aeronaut, and Mr. O. A. Gager are already here in St. Louis; and John La Mountain is now on his way here with a monster balloon.

Yesterday we had a conversation with Prof. Wise and Mr. Gager. They are very sensible men in every respect and seem to have no shade of doubt as to the success of their voyage.

Professor Wise is a man over fifty years of age, a resident of Lancaster, Pennsylvania, and an aeronaut by profession. He is a very quiet, undemonstrative gentleman; and, strange to say for a man who for twenty years has been advocating transatlantic aerial navigation, seems anything but a sanguine enthusiast.

Though positive that his views will eventually prevail, and aerial navigation become generally practicable, he is keenly alive to the mischances which await aerial voyages. It is difficult to realize after conversation with him that the cool, sober, practical man who converses so modestly of his exploits can be the foremost champion of a science which the public seems to consider purely visionary.

Mr. Wise is, at the present time, the most experienced aeronaut living. He says that "the dangers" the papers say he has run have been "purely imaginary." It is true that on one occasion when he was several thousand feet above the earth his balloon exploded, and he came down entirely out of control, the collapsed balloon and car whirling around in eddies and jagged circles. But the veteran aeronaut insists that this was nothing but a successful experiment, illustrating the capacity of collapsed balloons to act as parachutes.

"I must admit, that it was a moment of awful suspense. The gas rushed from the rupture in the top of the balloon with a tempestuous noise, and in less than ten seconds, not a particle of hydrogen remained in it. In another moment I felt a slight shock. Looking up to see what caused it, I discovered that the balloon was canting over, being nicely doubled in, the lower half into the upper; it had fallen, condensing the column of air upon which it was falling, until it had arrived at a point where it was so dense that the force of the whole weight pressing down on it was arrested, which caused the 'parachute' to tilt over. The weight of the car, however, countervailed the tilting tendency, giving it an oscillating motion, which it retained until it reached the earth."

He contends that at a distance of three to four miles from the earth there is a current of wind blowing from west to east, never varying in its direction and rarely in the rate of velocity. On this proposition he has experimented for years and has not failed once to observe this invaluable feature in the atmosphere. As soon as Prof. Wise discovered this phenomenon seventeen years ago, he conceived the idea that it was not impossible to navigate the air from America to Europe, and nurtured the design of some day making the experiment. In furtherance of this purpose, he applied to his friends for assistance but they hooted the project as crackbrained and nonsensical. He next petitioned Congress for aid:

"Your petitioner does not pretend to have discovered or solved any great newfangled problem; but from the improved state to which aeronautic machinery can be perfected, and the advantages continually at hand from the local currents of air, it is even now feasible to travel eastward with a velocity that will circumnavigate the globe in from thirty to forty days; with an ability to vary from a straight course thirty or forty degrees from the latitude of departure, which would enable us to leave dispatches in Europe and China, and return by way of Oregon Territory to Washington City.

"From these considerations, your petitioner is induced to ask your honorable bodies to make a naval appropriation to carry this project into practical operation."

But that body was too much engrossed in everyday affairs and paid no attention to him. Thus, he was forced to forego his cherished idea until some months ago when he associated with Messrs. Gager and La Mountain, the former the inventor of a balloon boat with air wheels and the latter a balloon builder of Troy, New York, and the united

energies of the three were brought to bear on the subject.

The Editor of the Troy *Budget* has taken a ride on the Hudson River in the lifeboat. He says it is a model of beauty, and, when beheld with its wings (the fans) beating above the water, looks like "a thing of life," a monster bird, wounded and fluttering in its efforts to rise to its native element, the ethereal regions.

They decided to make a series of experiments—one or two from St. Louis to New York, and if successful, then one from California eastwardly, and then from New York across the Atlantic Ocean. The three went to work immediately and earnestly, and in a few days we are to see what success is to attend the first trial.

The aeronauts say that their voyage is to be made at night, as by this arrangement, they secure daylight for the latter part of the voyage—a consideration necessary for the safety and success of the enterprise. To secure landmarks, a request will be made to ten different cities along either side of the route to keep their street lamps burning all night, with such forms of figures arranged by the lamps as to indicate the place so represented.

Mr. Wise considers Mr. La Mountain a practical aeronaut of great energy, and Mr. Gager a gentleman of nerve, courage, and clear head.

* * *

The names connected with this enterprise are significant. La Mountain—big thing—we like that. Wise —a quality quite requisite. Gager —rather suspicious.

TO THE EDITOR OF *Harper's Weekly:* I notice you make me the inventor of the "boat and power attached." Such credit justly belongs to Mr. La Mountain. We combined our ideas; but he has planned, directed, and built the aerial ship. Too much credit cannot be awarded to Mr. La Mountain for the energy and undying perseverance he has devoted to bringing about the completion of the enterprise. By correcting the item in reference to myself, you will confer a favor as well as award merit where it is justly due.

Truly yours,
O. A. Gager

TO THE EDITOR OF THE NEW YORK *Herald:* You cannot well imagine the astonishment created here in New York and at Lansingburg, by the publication in *Harper's Weekly* of a pretended illustrated history of the transatlantic balloon enterprise. I say "pretended" for no baser or more contemptible operation of the kind was ever attempted. The whole scope and object of the article was a glorification of John Wise, the Lancaster aeronaut, at the expense of John La Mountain, the projector and manager, thus far, of one of the most notable enterprises ever devised in the history of ballooning.

It is alleged that John Wise was the projector of the scheme for crossing the ocean. Mr. Wise, on the contrary, until within a few days past, had no connection whatsoever with it. He wrote to Mr. La Mountain last Fall, proposing a copartnership. The terms were unsatisfactory, and his offer was rejected. He then announced his intention of going forward with an individual enterprise, and Mr. La Mountain, under the supposition that this was being done, matured his plans and proceeded to manufacture his balloon. The model was his own; he selected the material; he arranged the disposition of the stuffs; he manufactured the varnish. In devisal and execution, he managed everything. There was no correspondence whatsoever between himself and Mr. Wise. From January to May, the parties were as strangers. The statement, therefore, that the Lancaster aeronaut directed the manufacture of the balloon is preposterous, as any resident of this locality knows.

Mr. Gager is simply the businessman of the enterprise—

nothing more. He is not a balloonist, and never claimed any acquaintance with the science of aerostatics. About a month ago a meeting took place in New York between O. A. Gager and Mr. Wise. At this meeting, Mr. Wise stated that some unfavorable remarks he had made in relation to Mr. La Mountain were based upon misapprehension, and asked to be admitted as a sharer in the enterprise. Mr. Gager had no authority to conclude an engagement, but wrote to Mr. La Mountain stating the proposition, and advising a concurrence, in the view of the long practical experience of Mr. Wise. Under these circumstances, Mr. La Mountain consented, and the veteran aeronaut became a copartner in the enterprise, without having invested a penny in it, or taken any part whatever in the labor performed.

Soon after, Mr. Wise came to New York. When he reached here, the balloon was finished, with the exception of putting the segments together; the boat had been built, and the propeller fans were nearly completed.

The "history" proceeds, that three voyages were projected by Wise, La Mountain, and Gager. *Mr. La Mountain* contemplates making three voyages—one from St. Louis this month, one from Chicago in August, and one across the Atlantic in September. In this his plans differ somewhat from that which "history" attributes to the veteran of Lancaster.

"The crew," the veritable narrative continues, "is to consist of Professor Wise, as director-in-chief, Mr. La Mountain as aeronaut, and Mr. Gager as navigator." I am authorized to say that Mr. La Mountain, the owner of the *Atlantic,* has made a slight change in these arrangements. The excursion from St. Louis will not come off on the 23rd, and when it does take place, the "director-in-chief" will be permitted to remain at home. It will not do to peril the life or health of a man in whom "history" has such a vital interest. As for Mr. Gager, he must be considerably amused by his designation as navigator. The gentleman has made but one balloon ascension.

Mr. Gager was not the inventor of the boat. It was built by Mr. Ingersoll, of New York, upon a plan furnished by Mr. La Mountain to whom credit is due for this as for everything else connected with the enterprise.

The "history" describes another balloon which it says was built by Mr. Wise. It has never been constructed, and perhaps the material of which it is to be constructed has not yet passed through the loom. At least Mr. Wise told this writer that he "had had such a scheme in contemplation, but had abandoned it upon his connection with Mr. La Mountain, and the balloon would not be made."

I send you herewith a history of the enterprise from the Troy *Times* of June 14 which does Mr. Wise full and ample justice:

"Mr. La Mountain selected the material. He made and applied the varnish, fabricated the twine, and made the netting. He devised the model and plan for his joint lifeboat and car. He invented and superintended the manufacture of the machinery. He has from beginning to end controlled this matter without any assistance, almost without advice.

"Mr. John Wise, the father of American aeronauts, is now connected with this enterprise. He first became so, less than a month ago. He was in this city about two weeks ago —finding the arrangements almost entirely completed. He declared with much emphasis that they were perfect in every respect, and had he been here from the outset, his long experience would not have enabled him to suggest any improvement whatever."

It is hoped that Mr. Wise had no hand in the preparation of the *Harper's* essay, though such an expression as "Mr. Wise desires us," etc., would seem to show the contrary. The matter is of no slight importance. Whether it succeeds or fails, the *Atlantic* balloon enterprise will become a subject of future history. It is of the first importance that its record should not be clouded by falsehood.

I have the authority to say that for the present, by the exercise of the power vested in Mr. La Mountain, the co-partnership with Mr. Wise is at an end. Unless he fully and in the most public manner disowns all connection with the unfortunate "history," he will not be permitted to enter the car of the *Atlantic* balloon.

One thing is very certain: Mr. Wise will not be permitted, under cover of a more extended reputation, to secure credit for what Mr. La Mountain accomplishes. Here, where all the facts are thoroughly understood by everybody, you can hardly conceive what a general statement of indignation has been excited by the publication of this fabulous history.

Geo. W. Demers

ATLANTIC

John La Mountain

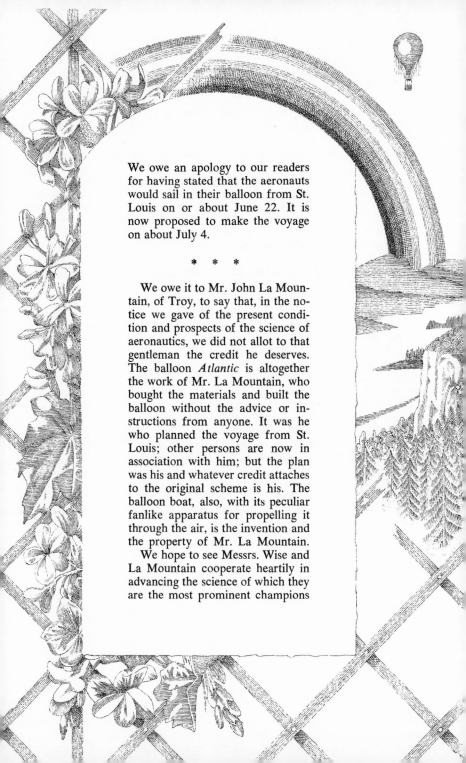

We owe an apology to our readers for having stated that the aeronauts would sail in their balloon from St. Louis on or about June 22. It is now proposed to make the voyage on about July 4.

* * *

We owe it to Mr. John La Mountain, of Troy, to say that, in the notice we gave of the present condition and prospects of the science of aeronautics, we did not allot to that gentleman the credit he deserves. The balloon *Atlantic* is altogether the work of Mr. La Mountain, who bought the materials and built the balloon without the advice or instructions from anyone. It was he who planned the voyage from St. Louis; other persons are now in association with him; but the plan was his and whatever credit attaches to the original scheme is his. The balloon boat, also, with its peculiar fanlike apparatus for propelling it through the air, is the invention and the property of Mr. La Mountain. We hope to see Messrs. Wise and La Mountain cooperate heartily in advancing the science of which they are the most prominent champions in the United States. It would be a disappointment to all who believe in them if anything diverted their attention from the main point which both have in view—namely, the development and the advancement of the business of air sailing.

* * *

We remember the time when the whole country was in a state of great excitement at the idea of steaming to Europe, which was accomplished just one month after a very high scientific authority declared that it was impossible. Now there is a controversy about ballooning to Europe, and two gentlemen each claim the credit of being the inventors of the machine or particular kind of balloon by which it is to be achieved. One of these adventurous spirits says he can do the voyage in two days. We would not wonder if, in the spirit of rivalry, both gentlemen should start in different balloons, that each should have his backers, and that heavy bets be staked on the issue. For our own part, we think a far safer and more ingenious way of reaching Europe is that which has been invented by an Irish genius in New York. He proposes to ascend to the upper regions until he is beyond the influence of gravity, and there wait till the world, revolving on its own axis, comes around to him, where he can just drop down on St. Paul's Church in London, in about twenty-four hours after he has ascended from Central Park; in coming back it will only take four hours, as the world revolves from west to east. This plan obviates the difficulty of steering balloons, which is the great drawback on their use. They have been used sometimes in war to bear messages, and to reconnoiter hostile camps; but that could only be done when the wind was favorable. By the new invention, the aerial voyageur ascends above the reach of the wind and weather, and has nothing to do but keep suspended in space until he is above the spot on earth on which he wishes to descend. The only danger would be that the daring aeronaut, in his efforts to get beyond the attraction of the earth, might be drawn into one of the volcanoes of the moon, and we should never hear of him again. . . .

Unknown Aeronaut

"Certain death, Mr.," says a greasy-haired rowdy before me, licking his yellow lips, as a vulture would grind his beak.

I followed the crowd down a winding walk to a space toward which all the other shady walks seemed to center. Inside the enclosure are two or three policemen, the French aeronaut, and several assistants. The balloon itself, folded in flat square sections, hangs from the ropeline stretched some forty feet overhead. It was constructed of that thin brown Manila paper which tradesmen use for their finer parcels; not grocery paper. Below, within the circle are a bottle and a tub full of straw; and the large wicker washing basket, says somebody, is the car.

The Frenchman, that little swarthy, apish man in the shirt-sleeves and white trousers, is actually now, ten minutes before he ascends, standing on two boxes looking over the vast area of paper, and stopping flaws with patches of pasted paper! Already, in five minutes, I have seen him caulk a dozen holes, and any one of these would have cost him his life. The myrmidons with a rope keep lowering and raising the balloon as he alternately wants fresh folds to examine or wishes removed what he has already inspected.

Now this being nearly completed, the brass band marches in and takes its place with mechanical joyfulness and triumph.

Creak goes the rope, up rustle the bales of paper, now the airship is erect, now it slowly widens and dilates—now it shakes forth its loose reefs, and globes out.

There is a sort of unrestrainable murmur of approval. The Frenchman performs some preparatory experiments. He produces some paper balloons; to one of them he ties a small tin tray full of spirits of wine. This he lights, and swift as a bubble in a long champagne glass, up goes the little fire ship. Away over the tall trees it skims, far, far away, burning tranquilly like a floating beacon in the windswept blue. Another buzz; the fire balloon has behaved most credibly, and deserves applause. But why lingers the Frenchman? Have we not all paid our 25¢ to see him die, and does the Gaul dare to hesitate?

No! He is but sending up another pioneer balloon to see which way the wind blows. It is all safe; the wind blows in from the Hudson toward the land. He will not be carried out to sea. Some treetop will catch him, or he will beat out his brains against some warehouse roof.

The wind is high, but it blows the right way. It is rather late in the year for balloon experiments, somebody in the crowd says regretfully; but if the breeze does not quicken, it is still a reasonably good day for an ascent. Now the Frenchman runs about in the ring like a newly caught mouse in a cagetrap, and prepares for the great moment.

He and his partners drag in the bale of straw, and close at hand the wicker car is placed, with its long cords ready to be attached. Excitement becomes painfully tense. The assistants drag at the foot ropes that hold the swaying balloon still tied fast at the top to the ropedancer's horizontal cord. The French- man, with a light, disappears inside the balloon, the neck of which is placed over the orifice of the tub which contains the lighted straw. The hot air from this straw will inflate the balloon, and render it as buoyant as gas. When full, the orifice will be tied up and the car attached. What is to become of the French Icarus when the heated air escapes? I find no one who can in- form me.

The balloon fills fast, its paper sides grow tense, the ropes are taut; in three minutes, somebody says, it will be time to fit the cork up. Even the smiling policemen are now busy in a brotherly way, hauling or tugging on the detentive ropes. Sud- denly, from inside of the balloon, comes the voice of the agitated Frenchman: "Fire! Fire! Get to me some water! Vite, vite, water! Give me!"

Instantly an overzealous policeman dashes a pail of water over the part of the balloon nearest to him, and it breaks through like blotting paper.

There is an angry laugh in the crowd, as if the whole thing were a trick. The Frenchman emerges, pale, stern, and fright- ened, and sets to work with paste and paper to patch up the large area of damaged surface. He explains that the inside of the balloon was not on fire, but that it was so heated that he feared it would ignite, upon which he called out "water" and the policeman, thinking it was on fire, instead of handing in the water, dashed it on the outside paper.

But the people are not satisfied.

"He never meant to go up at all," says one.

"Thunder!" says another. "If I haven't a good mind to go in and squash the darn bladder altogether."

"Let's all sail in," says an ugly customer.

In vain, the band struck up, for at that moment some rascal cut the rope, and down came fifty feet of paper in a rustling avalanche on the Frenchman and his loquacious assistants. Then a hearty laugh broke from the crowd, and all their anger melted in a moment.

I really pitied the poor Frenchman, as, heedless of the crowd's anger, he knelt over the hill of torn, wet, smoky paper, trying to drag it into shape and still patch it up for departure into space.

"Money, money," cried several voices.

But one of his assistants, a lean blackleg-looking man, will not let the moment of good humor pass again into anger. He leaps upon a table. . . .

"Fellow citizens! I guess you are all downright disappointed at this balloon not going up. I can assure you no one is more disappointed than my friend Monsoo Goujat, who has a bet of seven hundred dollars depending on this very ascent; but the wind is too high, I tell you, fellow citizens, and this accident now will prevent the ascent this afternoon. It will be necessary to cover the lower ten feet of the balloon with canvas or some uninflammable substance. But don't listen, fellow citizens, to anything anyone says, for this bully boy could go up now if we would let him. But we won't—no siree, we won't."

(Frenchman stamped and made a gesture of impatience and unsubdued will.)

"The ascent will, therefore, take place on this same spot— weather permitting—next Wednesday, at two o'clock and Monsoo Goujat, in order to convince you of the certainty of that ascent, will order your money to be returned to you at the gate where those who wish it may receive instead, tickets for admission next Wednesday." (Cheers.)

I suppose the weather did not permit, for I looked in Wednesday's newspaper and saw no mention of the paper balloon. . . .

CHAPTER 5

Professor Steiner and Monsieur Godard have a race . . . J. C. Belman attempts to beat both of them . . . Thurston is finally found — dead.

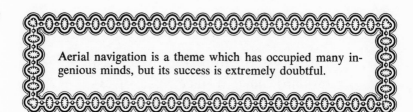

Aerial navigation is a theme which has occupied many ingenious minds, but its success is extremely doubtful.

Three Balloons in the Air at Once

BEAUTIFUL ASCENSIONS

CINCINNATI: The grand balloon race between Professor J. H. Steiner and Monsieur Eugène Godard drew an immense crowd to the vicinity of the City Lot yesterday afternoon. In the enclosure were some seven or eight hundred persons, but the surrounding streets were so choked up with people, horses, and vehicles, that it was impossible to move about. As many as thirty or forty thousand persons must have been in the neighborhood of the Lot.

Unknown Aeronaut

There it lies, a vast expanse of varnished silk, or calico, or india-rubber cloth, enveloped in netting, and covering many a square yard of ground with its flabby, crumpled form. Nothing more lifeless and uninteresting can well be conceived than the huge shape which, in a short time, will lift itself by degrees from the soil, like a giant creeping gradually into consciousness, and then will expand into one of the most stately and picturesque machines ever invented by man.

The balloons were inflated without any accident, and a little after four were ready for starting . . .

Now they enter the cars. The huge monsters above are swaying to and fro in the breeze, struggling for freedom like some giant souls which have done their work on earth and are eager to reach native skies . . .

Steiner

The day was beautifully fine, but a strong northwest wind was blowing, an accompaniment which appeared to amuse the spectators, who watched the flapping of the tents and the buffeting of my balloon.

As to the men holding on, they were liberally provided in every sense of the word, judging as I did by appearances, which included the color and expression of their faces, together with their gait and handling of the sandbags, which became less steady as the day wore on. This proved annoying, as it was just about the time that I depended upon assistance in checking the rolling of the balloon, which in all truth is sufficiently sweeping on a breezy day, without additional rolling motion on the part of the workmen through sheer inability to keep straight.

"Look out! she'll knock you down next turn!" cried one of the men, who had already annoyed me exceedingly, and was giving orders to his fellow workmen.

That thickheaded and mischievous workman, just as I ordered them to let up for the final test, facetiously exclaimed, "Let go," which some of them did, and I was so annoyed that I let go myself, not of the trigger, but my left fist straight for the nose of this dangerous assistant.

"Serves him right," exclaimed many voices, when the police dragged him out of the circle.

I then made another attempt to start, but what with the strong gusts and the stupidity of those who held the last connecting rope, a general rollover occurred. The moment a fresh chance presented itself I let her go, but was caught like a slow-rising bird at a pigeon match; that is, I received a full charge just as I was taking wing.

My car was quickly relieved of ballast to avoid a refreshment tent, but this did not clear her from the trees. Fortunately only the lower part of the balloon, with me in a crouched-down position, sustained a very sharp contact. A pathway was cut through, and I mounted rapidly. I then sprang onto the hoop and looked inside the balloon and saw nothing was amiss.

* * *

The parish church happened to stand in direct line with the course which my balloon was certain to pursue, and it was not very far away. I was all ready to duck low in the car in case of a collision, which took place just as I raised my head above the rim of the wicker protection.

For a moment every spectator looked on with alarm, and many shrieked as the balloon rebounded and again closed with the spire, and scraped up toward the top where, only a few days previously, had stood a large weathercock which, fortunately for me, had been taken down for regilding.

Having waved my cap as a signal that I considered—after a hasty inspection—that there was no rent, I heard a deafening cheer. . . .

Steiner and Godard then made their way upward, and moved off a little to the east in splendid style, and until after sundown were watched closely. Steiner took the lead, and when last visible appeared much higher than Godard. They will stay up as long as they can conveniently, which may be from one to three or four days . . .

* * *

About this time, Monsieur J. C. Belman took his aerial flight in the *Niagara*. He stated that it was his intention to go higher and farther if possible, than either of them. He had no doubt of his ability to remain up three weeks, and had serious intentions of going to the North Pole, and returning home by way of the Equator.

Belman will probably prove the greatest aeronaut living or dead, and will, we presume, be enabled in a few months to ascend unassisted by a balloon.

N.B. Since writing the above, Monsieur Belman has come down, having alighted about five o'clock at Glendale. At nine o'clock last evening on the corner of Fourth and Vine, he was visible to the naked eye, though some people insisted upon staring at him—greatly to the annoyance of his modesty—through smoked glasses and telescopes, regarding him as a celestial-terrestrial phenomenon, half comet and half eclipse.

The whereabouts of the other balloonists. . . .

* * *

They came down near Sandusky, at half past 10 and 11 P.M., of the same day, making some 250 miles, air line, in about seven hours, traveling 36 miles to the hour.

The Professor called upon us and gave a brief account of his aerial flight:

For the first half hour the balloons kept so close together that their occupants could converse; at one time so near as to cause a slight collision, which, however, did not injure either balloon . . .

At the start I was standing on the board attached to my car, but now I was sitting on it with my feet hanging down. He hailed me and said he was afraid his balloon would strike against my feet if he should suffer it to rise higher.

He was, of course, desirous to mount above me, and his balloon being larger than mine gave him some advantage in that respect. I told him he should not get above me if I could get ahold of his balloon, as I was determined to hold it down.

"It looks dangerous to see you sitting on that board."

"Never mind the danger, I'll be after you presently."

His balloon now stood about 200 feet from mine and a little above me.

"What do you think of the sight?"

"It's a magnificent one."

"I feel a breeze coming."

In another moment his balloon shot off southward . . .

I moved to different parts of the car; adjusted the furniture and apparatus; I uncorked my bottle, ate, drank, and wrote just as in my study . . .

I likewise ate the leg of a chicken; but my bread and other provisions had been rendered useless, by being mixed with the sand. . . .

After being up three quarters of an hour our adventurers parted company. Godard shortly after began to descend slowly until he nearly reached the ground and appeared to be making preparations to land.

At about 6 o'clock, Prof. Steiner lost sight of his companion at 3,000 feet. He then made preparations for spending the night in the clouds.

He ascended to an altitude of about 6,000 feet. Becoming very chilly and drowsy, he let down a drag rope of 3,000 feet in length, wrapped around his wrist, so that in case the rope dragged upon the ground, the jerking would awaken him—wrapped his shawl about him, and went to sleep. He remained unconscious until the balloon had sunk so near the ground as to lodge in the top of a tall tree, causing quite a concussion, upsetting the basket, spilling the provisions and two hundred pounds of ballast. The aeronaut awoke just in time to save himself from breaking his neck.

He righted up the balloon, which, now being lighter by the loss of so much ballast, shot upward, until it reached an elevation of about 12,000 feet. At this juncture, having lost nearly half his ballast and all his provisions, and knowing that in the course he was now sailing he would have to pass a stretch of water nearly one hundred and fifty miles wide before reaching the Canada shore, Prof. Steiner concluded to land on this side of the lake and made a safe descent, landing on the farm of Mr. C. Townsend, having been in the air six hours and twenty-five minutes. He spent the remainder of the night in a corn shock, where he was found next morning by Mr. Townsend, who kindly assisted in packing the balloon, and with whom the Professor breakfasted.

P.S. Since the above was written we understand by a telegram received that M. Godard landed at nearly the same hour as Prof. Steiner, in the neighborhood of Monroeville, and that he took the first train for Cincinnati. As the success of the aeronauts was to be determined by distance, it will be seen that Steiner is triumphant. Hurrah for Prof. Steiner.

* * *

We regret Prof. Steiner could not have stayed with us longer. As it was, he could barely call and report himself, and give, in hurried sentences, the particulars we have above reported. He started for Cincinnati—taking with him his balloon —on the 10:45 A.M. train.

THE LOST AERONAUT

Since the commencement of the search for the remains of Mr. Thurston in the swamps of Michigan and Canada, two bodies have been found, but neither was identified as that of Mr. Thurston. A correspondent of the Detroit *Free Press,* reflecting on his sad fate, has been induced to compute his mean velocity and momentum in falling to the earth. His elevation was thought to be three miles when he was last seen, and assuming this to be the distance he fell, and assuming his weight to be 160 pounds, he would strike the earth with a momentum equal to 160,800 pounds, or a little more than 80 tons—a mean velocity of 495 feet per second—a power sufficient to scatter his body, bone, and muscle into atoms, if not to bury him deep in the earth.

THE LOST BALLOONIST
Thurston's Body Found

CLEVELAND, MARCH 9TH: The body of Mr. Thurston was accidentally found on the 6th, about ten miles from the place of his second ascension. The remains were brought to Adrian and fully identified. The body was much decomposed, but a watch, money, and several articles easily recognized were found with the remains.

A pair of gloves was found in one of the coat pockets, and, in another, a letter and several cards. The letter, after drying, was readable, and was found to be directed to Mr. Thurston. It was from a Philadelphia house, in reply to some inquiries he had made about silk for a balloon.

Full Particulars

The remains of the lost aeronaut are found. They were brought to this city this morning. His coat, vest, pants, shirt, handkerchief, papers, memorandum book, blank slips or cards upon which his name is written, which he carried with him to record the incidents of the voyage, his pocket knife, and his watch.

A few of the bones were found, and all of them are in fragments. The skull is nearly entire, but the right parietal is crushed and a portion is gone. A portion of one of the thigh bones, nearly a foot long, and one of the bones of the forearm, five or six inches in length, are the largest bones brought here. There are besides several bones of the spine. The bones of the right leg and foot were found with the boot on, the bare bones of the leg sticking from the boot leg. The boot was cut off and the flesh of the foot and ankle was still adhering to the bone. These were so offensive that they were not brought here, but were buried near where the remains were found, about four miles northeast from Sylvania, on the farm of Mr. S. Miner.

The discovery was made last Sunday about sundown, by a lad named William Henry Hoag, fifteen years of age. The boy was ranging through the woods in search of his father's sheep when he discovered the coat and while stooping over to look at it, he saw the skull. He immediately went home, a distance of one hundred rods, and informed his father. Mr. Hoag returned with his son to the ground and found the clothes and some of the bones. The search was resumed on the following morning and other bones were found. Mr. Hoag suspected at once that they had found the remains of Mr. Thurston, and after further examination, was so well satisfied of the fact, that he placed the bones and clothes in a box and came this morning with it, to this city accompanied by his son and Mr. Miner. They inform us that numbers of hogs have ranged through the woods where the remains were found, and appearances indicated that the hogs and other animals had eaten and torn the body to pieces, and doubtless scattered the bones through the woods where others may yet be found.

It is now nearly six months since Mr. Thurston was lost. Mr. Hoag informs us that he has not now a particle of doubt that a young son of his saw the body when it came down on that day. The boy insisted at that time, and afterwards when everybody was searching for Thurston, that he saw a balloon fall, and he pointed out the direction of the place where it came down. On being asked now how he happened to see it, he replied that he heard a whistling noise and on looking up, saw it coming down. The whistling noise was doubtless made by the tremendous velocity of the body in descending.

There is not a particle of a doubt that these are the remains of Thurs-

ton. In addition to the evidence afforded by the papers found in the pockets of the clothes, Mr. Japheth Cross, who sold the watch to Mr. Thurston, has examined it and knows it by the number. The watch was run down, and stopped at 11:40. It does not seem to be injured, except that it is rusted. Mr. Cross has taken charge of it, and will clean it and put it in order when it will be presented to Mrs. Thurston, for whom it was purchased. The papers and memorandum book having been saturated with water for so long a time, are, of course, nearly destroyed, but they remain sufficiently perfect so that much of the writing is distinct.

Thus a mere accident has solved a mystery which, after this long time, nobody expected would be brought to light. . . .

* * *

Everyone who heard that the remains of the lost Thurston had been found and were coming into town, rushed into the street to get a sight of the men who were bringing the box, and to inquire concerning the circumstances. The box was carried into a room in the Balcony block, but the crowd there became so great that it was thought advisable to carry the box into the street before exposing the contents. This was accordingly done, and the articles of clothing were taken out separately and held up where the entire crowd could see. Each was greeted by exclamations of recognition.

The place where the remains were found is about ten miles from the point where he made his fatal ascent. It is quite probable that the balloon went in a direct line to the point where Thurston let go his hold, and that then the balloon rose to the current which carried it in a direction at a right angle with its first course, described at the time.

That the body was seen when it came down, by Mr. Hoag's little son, is generally presumed to be a fact. He called it a balloon, because he heard much concerning balloons at that time; and as it was no uncommon occurrence to see a paper balloon in the air, his father presumed he had seen one of that kind. The boy, it seems, saw it when he was alone. He ran immediately to an older brother and informed him; they then went together a short distance into the woods to search for it, but found nothing and returned. The next day when it became known that Mr. Thurston was lost, Mr. Miner met the boy and talked with him about what he had seen. From what Mr. Miner learned of the boy, he likewise drew the inference that the boy had only seen a paper balloon. Hence no search was made.

This explanation is necessary that our readers may not infer, from what was said yesterday, that Mr. Hoag and his neighbors were indifferent during the excitement of the search for Mr. Thurston. They perceived nothing in the boy's remarks that led them to suspect he had seen the body of Mr. Thurston. Besides, with very few exceptions, the entire community believed that Thurston was carried into Canada; and Mr. Hoag and his neighbors were looking for information of the body, if it should ever be discovered in that direction.

Wednesday, the remains that were brought here, together with the clothes found with them, were placed in a coffin, and after short religious services at the residence of Mrs. Thurston, they were followed to the grave by a few friends, without any parade, in accordance with Mr. Thurston's known sentiments while living and the wishes of his daughter.

CHAPTER 6

Accompanied by Wm. Hyde, a
newspaper reporter, Messrs. Wise,
La Mountain, and Gager have an
historic and frightening flight . . .
But is the science of ballooning advanced as a means of transporta-
tion?

A very large number of citizens of St. Louis witnessed a novel scene yesterday—that of the ascension of two balloons from Washington Square.

The crowds commenced gathering within the enclosure at one o'clock in the afternoon, but the usual heat of the day deterred the majority of spectators from reaching the grounds until four or five o'clock. The enclosure contained from six to eight hundred people, and the streets, open lots, board piles, and house tops were filled for squares around.

At four o'clock, we entered the grounds and found the inflation far advanced. It was the intention to fill the balloon to only one-half its capacity, which would leave plenty of room for expansion in the rare atmosphere of the upper region. . . .

GAS expands to double its bulk at three and three-quarters miles high, and to three times its bulk at five or six miles; to fill the balloon before starting would therefore be to waste gas, and possibly annoy the occupants of the car by its escape from expansion at the neck of the balloon.

During this process the liveliest interest was manifested by the spectators; and the aeronauts, sanguine more than ever of success, were keeping busy in discoursing with their friends on matters pertaining to the airship and the long voyage that they were about to embark upon.

The swelling volume of the balloon and its perfect proportion were admired, and the beautiful boat which was to carry the daring voyageurs was examined minutely. The operation of the wheels to be used in the management of the vessel was explained. Matters went smoothly and delightfully on until a noise occurred near the entrance gate, occasioned by a visitor insisting on making free use of a lot of wine which was provided for the aeronauts.

Mr. Baker, general superintendent of the grounds, interfered, but the thirsty individual insisted on helping himself to the wine. A scuffle ensued, in which the wine-bibber was vanquished, and soon after fell into the hands of the police. This little episode lasted but a few minutes. All became quiet again, and the interest in the legitimate business of the occasion resumed.

A peek in the boat and car revealed a strange medley. The most noticeable article was an Express bag, labeled as follows:

T. B. Marion, Agent, United States Express Company
22 Broadway
New York
This bag is sent from St. Louis by the aerial ship *Atlantic,* July 1. Please forward to destination from landing of balloon by Express, as above directed.
C. W. Ford, Agent
St. Louis

Besides this businesslike package, the cargo consisted of nine hundred pounds of sand in bags, a large quantity of cold chickens, tongue, potted meats, sandwiches, etc., numerous dark-colored, long-necked vessels containing champagne, sherry, sparkling catawba, claret, madeira, brandy, and porter, a plentiful supply of overcoats, shawls, blankets, and fur gloves, a couple or three carpetbags chock-full of what is called "a change"; a pail of iced lemonade and a bucket of water, a compass, barometer, thermometer, and chart, bundles of the principal St. Louis newspapers; cards of candidates for clerkships in several of the Courts, tumblers, cups, and knives, and perhaps other articles which have escaped me . . .

Five thirty o'clock arrived. Expectancy was high, and the balloon was pronounced officially inflated. Orders were given for the ring to be cleared. Two men were posted at each cord connected with the network of the balloon (so numerous were they that occupation was thus given to more than one hundred strong-armed men); the sandbags were unhooked from the meshes and the buoyant vessel rose from the ground. The airship was then towed from where it had been inflated, and the aeronauts stepped into the ring beneath it. Prof. Wise made a few appropriate remarks stating that he was not certain of success, as the ascension depended as much upon the friends around him as upon the aeronauts them-

selves. He requested those in present charge of the balloon to follow orders, which they all agreed to do. The boat was then brought into the ring and made fast beneath the capacious wicker car.

Mr. S. M. Brooks, an aeronaut of this city who had volunteered to escort, now unrolled his balloon the *Comet,* which was soon swaying in the air, impatient for a start into the blue ether. His light basket car was soon attached, and in the space of one half hour from the time the inflation commenced, the *Comet* with Mr. Brooks in his car was mounting upwards in beautiful style. The eyes of the crowd rested on it until its lone passenger was no longer visible, and then they turned with eager gaze onto the *Atlantic.*

Prof. Wise ascended into the basket, which was suspended about eight feet above the boat and within six feet of the hoop, so that the neck of the balloon would hang in the basket car whenever the balloon was fully distended. Messrs. La Mountain and O. A. Gager took their places in the boat, with Wm. Hyde, reporter for this paper . . .

Hyde

88

The aeronauts had very kindly allowed me to accompany them, on condition that if at any time my weight should prove an obstacle to the success of the voyage, I was to be landed —not thrown off as ballast, of course, but brought safely to the ground and exchanged for substance of lesser gravitation—while the others were to go on . . .

The crowd pressed about us in such a manner that to adjust the fanwheels of the machinery intended for raising and depressing the ship without the discharge of ballast and gas was found to be impracticable. Thus, the good people, anxious to perform any kind office, except to step a little to one side, delayed the ascension and compelled the aeronauts to relinquish any purpose the wheels might have served, as they could not be arranged in midair without risking life.

All arrangements being announced complete and everything ready, the largest aerial ship ever built ascended with four passengers, amid the cheers of the spectators, many of whom fully expect to hear of her landing on the Atlantic seaboard.

The most noted achievement recorded in aerial navigation, as regard to distance traveled, is the ascension of Mr. Clayton, made in 1833 in Cincinnati. That intrepid aeronaut was nine and a half hours in the air, and then descended in Western Virginia, three hundred and fifty miles from the Queen City. Mr. Wise and his associates have only to beat this exploit.

The ascension of the *Comet* placed at a quarter to seven in the evening, and that of the *Atlantic* at ten minutes to seven. They were grand sights to behold and the whole affair was a very superior order of this style of entertainment.

At the word, those who were holding onto the side of the boat simultaneously let go, and the Atlantic *rose slowly and majestically above the many thousands who were gathered in the vicinity, and sailed off. I have seen many assemblies, but never any to compare in number with the throngs which occupied Washington Square, which blackened the roofs of houses and the tops of lumberpiles, and who filled the streets. The applauding shouts of the people reached our ears for some time after we left the earth, growing fainter and fainter as we receded. When we no longer heard their voices, we ceased waving our hats, took seats, prepared ourselves to enjoy the sublimity of the varied scenery that presented itself upon hundreds and hundreds of miles around; and Mr. La Mountain announced that it was seven o'clock.*

The city of St. Louis was an imposing and magnificent spectacle. Large as I knew her territory to be, filled up with the most substantial evidence of commercial power and wealth, I had not formed any adequate conception of her real greatness from passing through her streets and viewing the mighty arteries throbbing with all elements of busy life and trade. As seen from above, a general appearance of squattiness conveys the idea—objects gradually become less clearly defined; the smoke from the foundries disappeared in the sky; streets grew narrower and darker; and finally the city faded into a spot.

By this time the barometer had fallen four inches, and the balloon commanded an extended view of the Mississippi, the Missouri, and the Illinois Rivers. I had the opportunity to realize (as much as possible to a practical person) the meaning of poetic dreamers when attempting to portray the silvery, glittering sheen of the waters, produced by the rays of the declining sun. Nothing should be imagined more gorgeously beautiful. We cracked a bottle on behalf of the silvery, glittery sheen of the water. . . .

The strips of timberland and fields of newly harvested grain of that portion of Illinois over which our silken globe was gliding were not grotesquely mingled as they might be supposed to, when viewed from a distance, but lay like a floor of mosaic ma-

sonry, regular and square. To our vision there were no hills or valleys, every object appearing set upon a level surface.

At ten minutes past seven o'clock, the barometer stood at twenty-four inches and the thermometer indicated fifty-five degrees. I now had the singular sensation described as the experience of all aeronauts on their first voyage. It was unpleasant and annoying, but by no means painful, very much a feeling one has while swimming; the ears become stopped up with water, making the tympanum grate rather harshly at any sound. The monster vessel had expanded a good deal since the ascension, and acquired a more rotund and symmetrical appearance. In a few minutes gas was blowing from the mouth of the balloon, the signal that it had become inflated to its fullest capacity. Prof. Wise, who had charge of the rope connecting the valve at the top, properly gave it a pull; and immediately a quantity of bluish vapor floated off and circled upward. This was at fifteen minutes after seven o'clock. A quarter of an hour later, the air ship had descended very considerably, the barometer indicating twenty-seven inches, the thermometer indicating sixty-five degrees.

We had been conversing about the magnificent scenery, relating anecdotes and watching with interest the progress of Mr. Brooks' balloon, the Comet. Every vestige of St. Louis had now vanished from our sight, and we were drifting at a wonderful rate of speed toward our far-off destination. I do not think I ever before experienced such an exhilaration of spirit—such real joy. Our motion was perfectly steady. There was no rocking of the boat or car, no rustling of the silk, nothing indeed, but the receding forests and fields beneath us to tell us we were not posed between earth and sky in a dead tomb. To have been apprehensive of danger would have been next to impossible. My feeling was that ballooning, besides being the most pleasant and swift, was the safest mode of travel known. Gliding down a rapid current in a boat on a lively evening with sublime bluffs, romantic caverns, and green foliage on either side, gazing at blue and mild sky above, is grand and delightful. Sailing on an unruffled lake, parting of placid waters, and skimming like a gull with gentle *sweetness, is ineffably glorious. But enjoyable methods of travel, I felt, yielded in point of dainty pleasureableness to the birdlike grace and impressive surroundings of aerial navigation with no breath of breeze stirring. The buoyant down of a thistle would have fallen to the boat by its own specific gravity. In all this calmness our monster bubble floated through the clouds. Twilight was on the earth, and gave off the odor of the soil, and the appearance of frozen lakes. By this time the sun had set to the inhabitants of the earth, though to us it was four or five degrees above the horizon. At thirty-two minutes after seven, we saw our companion, the* Comet, *which looked like a mere bladder, affecting a landing far to the northwest.*

At thirty-six minutes after seven o'clock, we were favored with a view of sunset, such as no painter could depict or any enthusiast describe. We were passing over the magnificent prairies of Illinois—those oceans of agricultural wealth—and the brightness of the western sky was in contrast with the oncoming darkness of the Mississippi and tributary streams.

During a twenty minute period we had descended rapidly, and to allow for this it was in turn requisite to open a bag of sand, dropping out a few handfuls. Thus we enjoyed the rather unusual occurrence of beholding the sun rise in the west—apparently rise, for the glorious luminary had only disappeared as our craft sank and came again in sight as the mysterious influence of the sandbag increased the distance between us and the earth.

Very gradually the darkness stole up from below. It was as though invisible hands were lifting up the veil as it approached, enveloping us. In a few moments the sun left us, disappearing in the hazy, luminous bank of red.

The barometer then stood at twenty-three inches and the weather was bitter cold. In spite of our shawls, overcoats, and gloves, our limbs were numb and our teeth chattered.

It was, I think, about this time that an incident occurred, both exciting and alarming. Prof. Wise had crouched himself down in the wicker car . . .

Wise   Mr. La Mountain proposed to take the lower current as long as it would take us but a few points north of east, and I told him to do as he deemed best and report his reckoning in the morning. After bidding the party in the boat a good night and Godspeed, I coiled myself up in blankets and lay down as best I could, and in a few moments was sound asleep, and knew of nothing but repose until 11:30 P.M.

Hyde   Mr. Gager had occasion to address some remarks to the veteran aeronaut, but received no answer. It was deemed impossible that he had fallen asleep so soon, and Mr. Gager again accosted him, this time in a louder tone. Still there was no response. A third and fourth time did he call; but heavy, deep, and convulsive breathing were the only results. Mr. Gager at once bounded to one of the upright irons of the fan-wheel machinery and clambered into the car. The balloon had become inflated to its fullest tension, and the professor lay immediately under its mouth. The expansion of the gas had driven some of the hydrogen directly into his face. He was, at that time, insensible, although as soon as the tube had been removed by Mr. Gager from its proximity to the professor's olfactories, and a few hearty shakes given him, the comatose man revived, rubbed his eyes, muttered a few incoherent syllables, and inquired about what brought his friend into the car and what was the matter. The profficient balloonist, who boasts of his two hundred and thirty-nine ascensions, had been taught a valuable lesson and took good care thereafter to keep the lower end of the gas bag out of the way of his smeller.

(While this was going on, the noble Atlantic had found the current blowing in the upper region, from the Occident to the Orient, and was now traveling toward the very star which they had picked out in the firmament as the beacon of the entire course they wished to take.)

There broke from Prof. Wise's lips a little cough; and saying, "Boys, let's sing," he struck up a stirring anthem, "Hail, Columbia," in which we all joined and carried through with a great deal of vigor and very little tune as the frigidity of the atmosphere put quite a damper on patriotism and melody. We kept along on this northeast current only a little while, however, as it was determined that the increase of our comfort would more than compensate for the loss of time in making the coast by lowering the vessel a considerable distance.

It was some time before it was ascertained what amount of gas would be necessary to discharge in order to depress the balloon to the proper point, there being no longer light enough to make any instrumental observation.

The aerial ship descended until the atmosphere ceased to be very cold; our party then began a siege on the eatables and drinkables, dispatching various good things—solid, fluid, and mixed—with alacrity and relish. About this time (a little after midnight), there were momentary flashes of lightning on all sides of the horizon. The Milky Way appeared like luminous phosphorescent clouds, and heaven's jeweled tiara of stars glistened below us and above. Night shimmered with the mellow light of the newborn crescent moon. Starlight and moonlight! Here was the poesy to which Shelley paid such deep adoration and which Alexander Smith delighted to cherish and to cultivate! Here was the mighty scroll of the cerulean-colored firmament glittering all over with gorgeous heraldry! We broke another bottle . . .

* * *

Large sources of light, betokening the presence of some more extensive community, would appear just looming above the distant horizon in the direction in which we were advancing.

By degrees, as we drew nigh, this confused mass of illumination would appear to increase in intensity, extending itself over a larger portion of the earth, assuming a distincter form and a more imposing appearance, until at length it would gradually resolve itself into parts, shooting out into streets which actually appeared to blaze with the innumerable fires wherewith it was studded in every direction to the full extent of all our visible horizon. . . .

The forms and positions of the more important features of the *city, the theaters and squares, the markets and public buildings, indicated by the presence of the larger and more irregular accumulation of lights, added to the faint murmur of a busy population, all together combined to form a picture which for singularity and effect certainly could never have been before conceived.*

* * *

At midnight, the whole dome of heaven was lit up. The stars shone with crystalline brilliancy, and the Milky Way looked like an illuminated stream of cumulus clouds. Whenever we crossed water this dome was as visible below by reflection as above.

Even at the greatest elevation we could discern prairie from woodland and from water. Lower down, by keeping the eye for a moment downward, we could see the roads, fences, fields, and even houses.

Gradually, as we drew nigh, these mysterious appearances would insensibly strengthen in their outlines, becoming more definite in their form, with an effect which I can only compare to that produced while looking through a telescope during the process of its adjustment, the confused and shadowy features of some distant prospect made to pass slowly through every gradation of distinctness ere the proper focus be at length obtained. We were floating in a sort of transparent vapor which, without possessing any perceptible body, seemed to be made up of luminous particles. The effect of this light was very peculiar. It gave the balloon a phosphorescent appearance, as though it were charged with fire. So powerful was this, that every line of the netting, every fold of the silk, every cord and wrinkle, was as plainly visible as if illuminated by torches; and I could at any moment tell time by consulting my watch. This phenomenon became more striking as we increased our altitude. My theory is that the clouds, charged with electrical particles and acted upon by the heat of the sun, emitted and dispersed through the air the luminous particles, which though separately indistinguishable, were still a myriad of torchbearers of our wondrous way. This theory has scientific warrant in the fact that ships have sometimes been similarly illuminated at sea, so powerfully that the masthead was visible from the deck, which would precede from the same causes, acting under different circumstances. It is not a natural feature of night, shown by the fact that when Charles Green, Mark Mason, and Lord Holland made their famous nocturnal voyage from London, it was so dark it seemed as if the balloon was passing through solid blocks of black marble.

96

* * *

At 12:35 o'clock we passed over a small river, but were unable to tell what it was, not being able to trace its course for a sufficient distance. At one o'clock we found ourselves sailing over a dense forest, and being quite low, distinctly heard the wind passing through the tree boughs, sounding like a heavy rain. We emerged from the woods—if the term is allowable—and floated over several habitations, which we saluted with our united voices . . .

Whenever we halloed it was followed by a distant echo, and even this served as a differential index to height. Only the dogs and bullfrogs had the kindness to send up their uncivilized acclamations, and these were always indicative of the fullness or sparseness of the habitations below, as we could hear them for many miles around us . . .

In return, we dispatched them the latest intelligence from St. Louis, done up in a copy of the Evening News, *as affording a sort of compromise between our language and theirs . . .*

Mr. La Mountain remarked that nobody lived in that country but dogs, or else people barked like dogs, he having got a little out of humor because nobody would tell him in what State we were sailing, and he gave up the inquiry.

At 1:30 we glided over another river and canal, and thirty minutes later over a railroad track. The river was doubtless the Wabash, and the railroad the New Albany and Salem. If there was but one truly crooked river in the world, no person going over the Wabash, attached to a balloon, would hesitate to say that was it.

Prof. Wise and Mr. Gager had been asleep since about half past twelve o'clock. I had taken about an hour's rest in broken doses having been in a dilemma whether to close my eyes or keep them open for passing events. The quandary was settled by my coming to the conclusion that such trips as the Atlantic *was making were by no means of everyday occurrence and it would not do to miss any of the incidents.*

Mr. La Mountain who had been very jovially inclined during the early part of the night, suddenly became rather indisposed to talk, and I observed him bowing with closed eyes at the bottom of the boat. He had worked with great industry getting the cords, valves, etc., in trim for the voyage and had taken but little sleep. While he was dozing, I observed a current of air taking us downward and called his attention to it. We had just time to scoop up a couple of hands full of ballast apiece and drop them overboard to save us from a collision with a clump of trees which stood in alarming proximity. Such was our nearness to the earth at this time that we distinctly heard the sand strike upon a roof top. Presently a sprinkle of gas lamps twinkled forth, and then we heard a shouting, and ascertained that we were over a small town, probably in Kath County. The balloon, once more freed from a portion of her freight, darted up again and went above the branches without touching, although the margin was quite small.

It was twenty minutes to three o'clock then. Dawn was just tinging the East with a faint purple glow; and at three o'clock I could distinguish where there was a line in my notebook, sufficiently to avoid making one memorandum directly over another.

*During this period all three of my companions were fast asleep
(the atmosphere being very warm and pleasant at the altitude we
maintained), and their decided snoring gave me pleasing accompaniment in my voyage and somewhat varied my reflections. It
thus developed on me to be "scientific director," "navigator,"
and "aeronaut," in one; the responsibility of which I flatter myself was not misplaced, inasmuch as there was nothing for me to
do except to wonder how far we had traveled, what course we
were taking, where we were going, and when we would get there;
duties that I performed with astonishing proficiency, for a novice.
I called out always on a passing house, and was invariably answered by the bark or howl of a dog.*

*We were now gliding majestically through the clear ether. I
kept the balloon within four or five hundred feet of the earth—
using during that time but three pounds of ballast, which I considered a little remarkable. I observed the same combination of
forests and fields into regular squares that had attracted my attention in the early part of the evening while above Illinois.
Every object was dressed in an emerald hue.*

*At this time, daylight made its appearance, heralded by a faint
glimmering in the East, quickly followed by a brilliant illumination of the whole vista of space in which we were moving. Again,
the veil seemed to move over us, hung for a short time between
the balloon and earth, and then disappeared, as if its particles
had decomposed and floated away. Now the splendid panorama
lay spread out beneath us and all was gleaming. It seemed as if
every tree bore a coronal and every field of grain was headed
with a cabinet of gems, while the surface of waters shone with
untold magnificence. I could not refrain from exclaiming aloud.*

*At 3:35 o'clock we floated over a village composed of a dozen
or more houses in a pretty cluster. By this time all the party were
awake and lively. We transacted a little business with the instruments at our disposal, jotting down height, temperature, hu-
midity, and other facts and figures; then we chatted, ate, and
sang till sunrise at 4:15 o'clock, when we left to the right of us a
large town which Mr. La Mountain said was Ft. Wayne, Indiana.*

CINCINNATI, JULY 2ND: The balloon
passed six miles north of Ft. Wayne at
four o'clock this morning. The small balloon was seen at that time a considerable
distance north.

*We could plainly hear the shouts of the astonished and de-
lighted inhabitants, and Mr. Gager let go with resounding and
jolly Hurrahs, given then by the whole of us with a will. It is not
probable that we were heard. We threw off some papers and bills
of fare at Barnum's Hotel which may have alighted within ten
miles of the town.*

*Twelve minutes after five we descried in the East what at first
appeared to be the reflection of the sun in the sky. The noble air
vessel was wisping along at a brisk rate, dragging its shadow on
the ground encircled in fantastic colors. Groups of white clouds,
like great puffs from a steampipe, floated languidly on every side,
unfolding their gauze-like robes and passing off in eddying currents. We could hear the lowing of cows with distinctness.*

*A fine light silk umbrella marked "Geo. Davis" had been left
in the boat by some person in Washington Square. Unfolding it,
I had an excellent protection for myself and Mr. Gager from the
heated yellow rays which were now pouring in on us.*

*There was no doubt now that what had at first seemed a bril-
liancy of the eastern heavens was nothing less than an immense
body of water—Lake Erie with its surface of 7,800 square miles;
and though we could not behold the whole of it, the view lost
none of its magnificence. There was a collection of houses hud-
dled together where the Maumee River pours its tributary into
the lake, and this was Toledo.*

*We were low enough to distinguish objects the size of men,
and, as the balloon darted above houses, we could plainly discern people and hear their voices. One apprehensive individual
yelled out, "You'd better watch out. That's the lake!" Another
contented himself with the exclamation, "Hoo–e–e!" Seven*

o'clock saw the gallant Atlantic parting company with the shore, a little north of Port Chilton, then making due east.

As we emerged upon the lake, a little steamboat that was propelling up a river headed for our track, and someone aboard her cried aloud to us, "That's the lake ahead of you!" Mr. La Mountain cried back, "Is it Lake Erie?" and the answer was, "Yes it is, and you'd better look out!" Our good friend rounded off again, sounded us a goodbye with his steam whistle, and went his way up the river, leaving two long, beautiful wings of foam behind.

A small propeller did the Atlantic the honor to blow her whistle, and immediately hove to, her commander doubtless imagining we were about to descend into the water where he would have to pick us out. A considerable quantity of ballast was now discharged, and as of 7:25 o'clock we swept by Sandusky City; the barometer shot up to twenty-three and a half inches, the thermometer indicated fifty degrees.

SANDUSKY, JULY 2: The aerial ship *Atlantic* passed here at 7 o'clock this morning. Its course was east by south. A paper was dropped from it, but it fell unfortunately into the lake. Only three persons were visible. The name of the ship was distinctly seen.

The balloon, having reached the rarefied regions, expanded almost to its full capacity and again it was found necessary to pull down the safety valve and let off gas. By this time we had sailed far from the shore, and the lake appeared dotted for miles with white objects which we knew to be schooners, the light glistening upon their sails, making them seem as though they were so many beams of sunshine standing like arrows in the water.

At Mr. La Mountain's suggestion—that we could make the city of Buffalo by sailing but a few hundred feet above the surface—the valve was opened until we gradually sank to within *five hundred feet of the water. Here we found a gentle gale of a mile per minute and we resolved to float on it until we should be in sight of Buffalo, then rise and sail over it.*

At 8:30 o'clock Prof. Wise directed more ballast to be thrown overboard. The alarm which suggested this was soon over, however, and at 9 o'clock the whole party were as merry as when they were lifted toward the clouds at starting.

> CLEVELAND, JULY 2: The balloon passed Fairport, thirty miles east of this point at 9:30 A.M. and was seen to nearly touch the water. It rose again and disappeared in a northeasterly direction.

At half past nine o'clock we overtook a steamer bound for Buffalo. The decks of it were crowded with persons whose huzzas were borne to our ears, attended by the shrill scream of the boat's steam whistle.

We were wafting along in a northeasterly course, making decidedly the fastest time on record. At six minutes of ten o'clock, the steamer could be faintly seen on the horizon, so rapid was our flight. The balloon was passing then over Long Point. Soon we had traversed nearly the entire length of Lake Erie, a distance of 250 miles, accomplished in three hours!

At half past ten o'clock we had Lake Erie and Lake Ontario both in sight. The balloon had now attained an altitude of nearly a mile. A terrible storm was surging beneath us, the trees waving and the waves dashing against the shores of Erie in a tempestuous manner. But above the careening whirlpools and the thundering breakers swam the proud Atlantic, *not a cord nor a breadth of silk disturbed, soaring aloft with her expectant crew, gaily heading for the salt crest which bounds our vast Republic. The barometer marked 23.6 inches.*

* * *

We were scurrying along the Canada shore, passed near the mouth of the Welland Canal, and soon began to mount for our more easterly current so as to take Buffalo in our track, but we circled up into it, between Buffalo and Niagara Falls, crossing Grand Island, leaving Buffalo on the right and Lockport to the left, rushing on our course. Here we had a view of General Braque's monument, Queenstown, St. Catherine's, Gravel Bay, Lewiston, Black Rock, Fort Erie, and other celebrities of that locality. Now, like a gurgle, comes the subdued roar of the crashing and headlong Cataract of Niagara.

The famous Falls were quite insignificant seen from our altitude; a descent of about two feet and the water seemed to be perfectly motionless. The spray gave to the whole an appearance as of ice, and there was nothing grand or sublime about it.

NIAGARA FALLS: We scarcely thought when penning a pleasantry in Saturday's paper that the balloon would pass over this place. On looking at the map, it would seem that it is considerably out of the most direct course to the Atlantic. We are prepared now to believe most anything.

At 11:45 A.M., some of our citizens discovered the balloon a little south of the village pursuing a northeasterly course. Some estimates said it was five to six thousand feet in the air. They saw the car and almost saw the voyageurs. It soon passed out of sight in its rapid course. This voyage throws into shade all previous efforts of the kind.

Passing the western terminus of the Erie Canal, the balloon was borne directly toward Lake Ontario. Our ballast was now nearly exhausted, and to have determined on crossing the second lake would have been sheer recklessness and hardihood. At this point it was resolved to descend to the earth, land Mr. Gager and myself, in our stead take in a sufficient quantity of new ballast, and again steer to a point in Boston.

The airship was lowered, but was immediately caught in the hurricane which was then raging, and carried very near the tops of trees which were bending and swaying to and fro by the force of the wind. The surface of the earth was filled with clouds of dust. Mr. La Mountain at once threw over the buckets and their contents, and the lift this gave kept us from being caught in the woods.

Like a bullet we shot out into the lake. The waves roared like a host of Niagaras. We overtook seven steamboats, passing mutual salutations, and would soon leave them flitting on the horizon in our rear. One of these lonely travelers remarked as we passed him, "You're going it like thunder!"

Wise

Mr. Hyde looked up to my car, and very solemnly said, "This is an exciting time, Professor. What shall we do?"

"Trust to Providence and all our energies," said I. We were fast running farther onto Lake Ontario, and how terribly it was foaming, moaning, and howling. I said, "La Mountain, I have one hundred and fifty pounds of ballast in my car yet and a heavy valise, an Express bag, and lots of provisions."

"Well," he said, "if that won't do, I'll cut up the boat for ballast, and we can keep above water until we reach the opposite shore" (which was nearly a hundred miles off the direction we were then going).

La Mountain

I said, "You must all get into the basket if you want to be saved, should we ever reach the land. But I truly tell you that the perils of the land are even more terrible than those of the water, with our machines; and it would be easier to meet death by drowning than to have our bodies mangled by dashing against rocks and trees."

Mr. Hyde said very coolly, "I'm prepared to die, but I'd rather die on land than in the water."

I said, "What do you say, Mr. Gager?"

He replied, "I'd rather meet it on land, but do as you think best."

Mr. Hyde said to me, "I guess we are gone!", and with a despairing countenance climbed up with Wise and Gager in the basket, leaving me alone in the boat.

It was a desperate time, but I cannot say I was disconcerted. I had seen worse perils of the same sort before. My only thought was that at a point on the shore dimly visible from where I stood, my mother lay buried.

Wise looked over the basket and shouted, "For God's sake, La Mountain, throw overboard anything you can lay your fingers on!"

I knew Mr. Wise was excited, and I did not care to waste my ballast so high above the water.

Hyde

No sooner had I planted myself firmly in the wicker basket than down, down with fearful speed went the huge Atlantic *toward the lake. I closed my eyes involuntarily but was quickly aroused by a crash and a lunge of the car forward. Three times was there a terrible clatter and splash. One moment more of life, thought I . . .*

La Mountain

The effect of striking the wave crest was the same as a descent would have been upon a sharp pointed rock. I was holding on by the ropes when the shock came. Its force was so terrific as to dash in three planks on one side of the boat—but the water was prevented from coming in by the strong canvas on the outside. After the concussion, we bounded fifty or sixty feet, like a rocket shot. I was jerked by the shock, so that my head hung over the water. My beaver fell off, and my watch guard was broken square in two . . .

Hyde

Looking around I beheld a hat floating off, and the same instant the balloon darted out of the water. I thought La Mountain gone . . .

"For God's sake, John, are you out?" Wise shouted over the basket.

"Don't trouble yourselves about me, gentlemen," was the response. "I'm all right and I'm going to take you across safe yet."

La Mountain

My companions were excitedly calling out to me on all sorts of subjects, but I paid as little attention as possible to them. After we escaped the first shock, I felt perfectly confident that we would come out safely and told them so, but they hardly seemed to believe me.

We had gotten far out, and there was now no land in sight. A dreary waste of nearly seven thousand miles of water was before and around us. For awhile we cherished the hope that we would be able to pass the broad expanse of deep in safety. But this hope died out in less than an hour as the trooping winds bore down on us, it seemed with increasing fierceness.

At length, we again neared the dashing billows which were wildly flinging up their white caps and chasing one another toward the northeast. For me, a lifetime was concentrated in that awful moment. It was the first time since I had set foot in the boat that I had experienced fear as to my safety. I looked at my companions; they were calm, but their countenances gave me no assurance. I knew, if I should climb into the basket with the others, we should all be drowned together; and I was determined not to be drowned if I could help it. I pinned my watch in my pantaloon pocket, thinking that if we were drowned my body might be washed ashore and my wife would get the keepsake. I hoped that by clinging to the boat and cutting it up piecemeal, we might be saved . . .

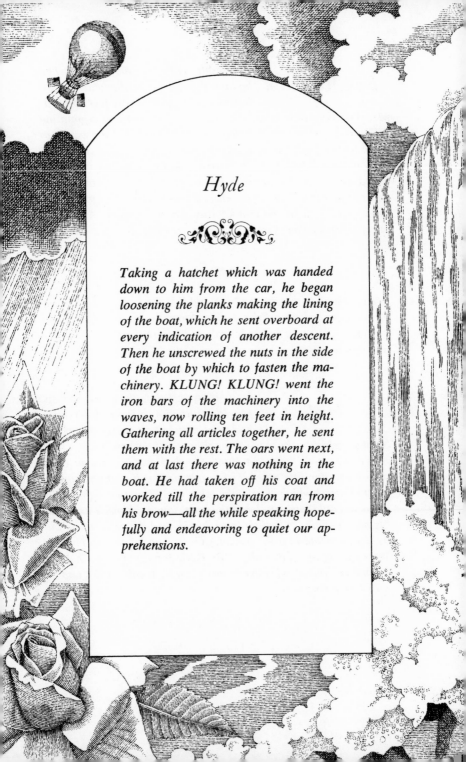

Hyde

Taking a hatchet which was handed down to him from the car, he began loosening the planks making the lining of the boat, which he sent overboard at every indication of another descent. Then he unscrewed the nuts in the side of the boat by which to fasten the machinery. KLUNG! KLUNG! went the iron bars of the machinery into the waves, now rolling ten feet in height. Gathering all articles together, he sent them with the rest. The oars went next, and at last there was nothing in the boat. He had taken off his coat and worked till the perspiration ran from his brow—all the while speaking hopefully and endeavoring to quiet our apprehensions.

La Mountain   *The result verified my anticipation. The balloon did not strike the water again, but varied from six to fifty feet above it. Mr. Wise here proposed to descend into the lake and swamp the balloon—in other words, to leave us at the mercy of the waves, to swim forty or fifty miles to shore! He must have made this proposition thoughtlessly. I, of course, preemptorily declined it. I called to my companions to hand me down their carpetbags, valises, and mailbag, and other articles which I successively threw into the lake and that kept us above the water. A moment later, the propeller* Young America *was signaled and asked to lie to. . . .*

*   *   *

I proposed to swamp the boat and balloon in the lake trusting to being picked up by the Young America. *As we crossed her bow, they gave us a hearty hurrah, but before she could lie to she was a mile astern . . .*

Hyde   *Happily by this time the shore had appeared in the dim distance. Everything had now gone but an overcoat and two blankets which were saved to be used as a final resort.*

We skimmed thirty feet above the dark waves for a distance of not less than fifty miles. The hurricane was blowing us toward a dense forest which skirted the lake. (La Mountain right at this moment could have cut loose the boat, landing himself and leaving his companions to their fates; but instead, he drew himself up by the rope and into the basket.) Overcome by admiration, Mr. Wise sprung up, exclaiming, "By God, John, you are a hero! If I can come out of this alive, you shall have a gold medal and the credit of saving us all!"

La Mountain *I saw by the swaying to and fro of the lofty trees into which we must inevitably dash, that our worst perils were at hand. I ordered two men upon the valve rope, and we struck within a hundred yards of the water, hurling through the tree tops at a fearful rate . . .*

Hyde *Mr. Gager had thrown out the heavy anchor. So rapid was our flight that this stood out nearly straight from the car. As the anchor swung against the trees of moderate size, the velocity of the balloon and its terrible strength would break them off and fling them to the ground like pipestems. One by one the anchor hooks broke off, and we were at the mercy of the all-sweeping wind. Mr. La Mountain and I held onto the valve rope, endeavoring to discharge the gas; but we quickly were compelled to release our grasp and cling to the concentrating hoop to avoid being thrown out. The enormous balloon pursued its resistless course, breaking branches, dashing our car to and fro against tree trunks and limbs, until the stout netting had broken little by little and the bag itself no longer had any protection . . .*

* * *

After dashing along this way for nearly a mile, we plunged most fearfully into the boughs of a tall elm, so that the basket swung under and up through the crotch of the limb, while the boat had caught in some of the other branches. But in another moment the Atlantic *puffed up her huge proportions, and at one swing, away went the limb, basket, and boat into the air a hundred feet. This limb, weighing not less than six or eight hundred pounds, proved too much for the* Atlantic, *and it brought her suddenly down upon the top of a very tall tree. The silk was punctured in a dozen places and rent into ribbons, leaving the car suspended by the network some twenty feet above the ground, dangling in the most sorrowful-looking plight of machinery that can be imagined . . .*

* * *

It is difficult to see how any one of the quartet escaped with his life. It happened that the landing was made within a hundred and fifty yards of a settlement. A number of farmers had observed the balloon rushing along over the forest, and of course at its crash the people ran to the spot. Singular as it would appear, there was only one of the four injured in the least—Mr. La Mountain receiving some slight contusions about one of his hips.

* * *

When we got down, which was done partly by ropes and partly by means of the broken tree, several persons were standing around with open mouths, and eyes staring in wonder. . . .

* * *

About twenty men and young girls surrounded us and had a million questions to propound relative to the extraordinary voyage, but we soon got used to that sort of thing.

We then learned that we had landed on the place of Truman O'Whitney, near Sackett's Harbor, in the township of Henderson, Jefferson County, New York. By Mr. La Mountain's watch, the time was two o'clock and twenty minutes. We had been nineteen hours and thirty minutes traveling a distance which cannot be computed at less than nine hundred miles, and is said to reach as much as twelve hundred miles.

In the bottom of the car we found a couple of copies of the St. Louis Price Current *and the card of Fred Karetscamar, candidate for the office of Clerk of the Criminal Court. After the natives had somewhat recovered from the surprise we were beset on every side with requests to accompany all of them home.*

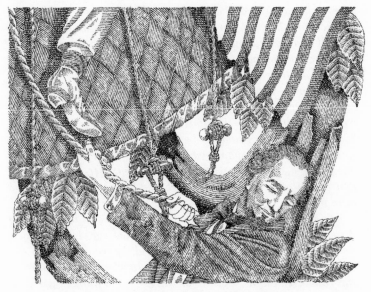

We finally went to the house of Mr. Justice Wayne, not a great way off, where the women folk set about to give us a first rate dinner.

Having finished our meal and being anxious to let our friends know of our safety, we inquired the way to the nearest telegraph station, which was at Adams, ten miles distant, on the Watertown and Rome railroad. Mr. Wayne geared up a team for Mr. Gager and me, while a neighbor performed a like service for Prof. Wise and Mr. La Mountain. On the road to Adams, one of Mr. Wayne's acquaintances met him and asked if he had heard about the air balloon which had alighted in the woods. A glow of pride and complacency spread all over our driver's honest phiz, and he replied, with an affirmative shake of the head, "Yes, and here's two of the men that was in it!" The foot traveler felt immediately that he had been eclipsed.

On our arrival at Adams, we made our business known at the telegraph office without delay and sat down and prepared dispatches. A half a dozen loungers gathered about us, and as they were civilly answered, the news spread like a prairie on fire. We had scarcely finished our messages when each one of us found himself surrounded and had to go through the entire account.

One after another came up, each wanting us to repeat the whole narrative from the beginning. They hesitated to believe

that a journey had been accomplished in their country from so remote a region as St. Louis, in less than twenty hours. Some excuse may be found for their incredulousness in the fact that they had recently been swindled by a miserable hoax concocted by some ingenious newspaper editor, relative to the descent of an imaginary meteor somewhere in that vicinity. It was suggested that the aerolite was nothing more nor less than a bag of sand from the Atlantic *balloon.*

Some gentlemen remarked that it might be well for Professor Wise to address the multitudes. The professor, in obedience, gave out that if a hall could be procured, he would relate a history of what our party had done and seen; whereupon, a meeting was concocted on the spot. In half an hour, the whole town knew of Prof. Wise's promise, and soon a commodious room was jam-filled with ladies and gentlemen anxious to hear all about it. So the veteran Wise, Mr. Gager, and I (Mr. La Mountain had returned to look at the wrecked balloon) were trotted out on a large platform, a President and Secretary appointed, and Prof. Wise proceeded to relate an interesting account of the voyage. When he concluded, Mr. Gager was called on, and made some appropriate remarks relative to the cold shoulder which is usually turned to projects of importance in their infancy. Both gentlemen stated their entire satisfaction with their experiment and that they were more than ever convinced that the science of aerostation would yet amount to something which would astonish the world.

The journey is the longest one by far ever made. Prof. Wise announces that if he can raise the requisite means he will immediately undertake to sail an aerial ship across the Atlantic Ocean.

*   *   *

These narratives of that remarkable aerial voyage have an attraction all their own and cannot fail to stir up excitement and awaken admiration in the hearts of all who read them. Intrepidity and daring are not restricted to the battlefield; and those qualities appeal as much to our recognition and applause when exhibited in any other field of human action.

These aeronauts will by no means consent to have their deeds recorded among the useless. They cling to the belief, and they assert their convictions with a confidence that inspires respect, that with their aerial ship they can cross the ocean safely, expeditiously, and with much precision as to their course.

Mr. Wise said that it would have been quite easy for them to have sailed directly to the city of New York, as it was proposed, had they kept more in the upper current; but that the plan was frustrated on account of the unpreparedness of some of the crew for so cold an atmosphere. We do not know whether this is reconcilable with Mr. La Mountain's statement that the upper current—a two and a half mile distance above the earth—was blowing in the same direction as the

hurricane. Both agree, however, as to the theory of there being uniform currents at certain altitudes. While their balloon, at an altitude of a mile and a half, was carried along in an easterly direction, a smaller balloon lower down, which had undertaken to pilot them over St. Louis, was not carried in the same direction.

Both declared themselves well satisfied with the result of the experiment and more than ever determined to go forward with the enterprise of transatlantic ballooning. At all events, this has been the most remarkable and successful experiment that has yet been made in aerial navigation, and the narratives of the voyage are most exciting.

In such an age of wonders as ours, we do not choose to risk an unblemished reputation for prophecy, by predicting that aerial navigation as a useful science is an impossible thing. But we may safely say that this last balloon voyage from St. Louis proves nothing except that man is a very puffy animal, and that ballooning is now as it always has been—one of the most certain methods of showing how ready he is to brave all dangers, even the risk of being dashed to pieces, smashed out of all semblance to humanity by a fall of a mile or two, or drowned like a kitten in a basket, in the hope of doing what was never done before. As all balloon voyageurs show this cool and indomitable courage, the difference between Mr. Wise and his companions in this last one is a difference not so much in kind as in degree. They have done more than was ever done before, inasmuch as they have traveled further by about six hundred miles; and they have made quicker time than was ever made before for any great distance. They also went in the general direction intended, but this others have done before them.

Distance and speed, then, seem to distinguish this voyage from all others accomplished by previous navigators of the upper air, and in distance and speed alone have these men triumphed. . . .

CHAPTER 7

The Glorious Fourth . . . How our country's Independence is celebrated in Jones' Woods . . . A political speech . . . One of the stellar attractions never leaves the ground. But if it had, what wonders you would see.

MESSRS. FOX AND LINGARD

ANNOUNCE FOR TODAY

A SERIES OF OUTDOOR ENTERTAINMENTS

AT JONES' WOODS. . . .

The noisiest city in all Christendom today is New York. Italy, bristling with arms and echoing to the explosions of gunpowder in earnest, is enjoying the Sabbath stillness compared with the hubbub and confusion, clatter, bang and racket, whiz, roar and thunder of New York, uproarious and reverberating with gunpowder on a frolic. No wonder then that 10,000 people whose ears are not attuned to the rough music of rampant juvenile patriotism will rush out today, deep into the country, by steamboats—sinking their decks to the water's edge—and all railroads, hoping to escape some of the overwhelming confusion to which the city is surrendered.

The stranger who should land in New York today, quite ignorant of American history and manners, would certainly never imagine that he was assisting at the most august festival of a great people, busy in doing honor to the wisdom, courage, and constancy of their fathers, and in expressing their gratitude for the magnificent fortune which has followed the steady expansion.

It is the day of excursions—and for a hundred miles around the metropolis, the usually quiet streets of all accessible villages will be swarming with men and women, babies in arms, and elaborately dressed clerks bearing light mustaches and tenderly guarded meerschaums.

A word to the Excursionists: Take along a large supply of patience, and plenty of sandwiches. In the cars there will be dust in spite of the late showers, or at least cinders, smoke, a crowd, abundant perspiration, and considerable thirst.

> It would be easily possible for us to make the Fourth
> of July a real Saints' Day in our national calendar, and by
> keeping it as a high festival in some noble and worthy way,
> to use it as a powerful agency in behalf of the civilization of
> America. . . .

118

On the steamboats, there will be apparent swindling about return tickets, little boys popping off firecrackers, unmannerly elbowing, looseness of conversation, and occasional profanity. Then uncork your bottle of patience and take a long pull at it. The draught will revive your spirits, make the elbowings mere evidence of sociability, and convert the crowd into a jolly democratic union.

All demure, peace-loving people confess the Fourth of July, as at present maintained, to be a bore. But as it saves the Union, and as the smell of gunpowder with which it is redolent, nurses valor in the hearts of youth, it should be celebrated.

Because it is celebrated, fetched out from the common run of days, and distinguished as memorable, it is of little consequence what the method is. If, then, your excursion train should happen to come in collision, put down the broken legs, detentions, and the disappointments, as a sacrifice to the Spirit of Freedom.

So you of the little carpetbag and satchel, today rejoice in whatever turns up; make the most of your sniffs of ocean air and whiffs of country breezes; of your glimpses of rural beauty and your hours with nature. Be jolly if circumstances permit, and if they don't, be thankful for so early an opportunity to put behind you a few more of the annoyances you were fated to meet on your journey through life. At any rate, hurrah for the day we celebrate.

* * *

Jones' Woods are not Elysian fields. Romance and poetry dwell not therein. Tranquil delights have there no abiding place. Of sheltering shades, and balmy breezes, and languishing lawns, and other rural comforts which woodland and grove are popularly supposed to afford, there are limited supplies. Of bustle and tussle, broil and hurly-burly there are profusion and variety. You would perhaps expect nothing else in a place with such a name. Jones does not awaken hopeful expectations. There is nothing about Jones to appeal to your tender imaginations any more than about Smith, Brown, or Robinson. Jones' Woods is simply a businesslike title: meritorious in brevity, and exceedingly apt in application. For Jones' Woods, especially on Sundays, is about the most businesslike place you have visited.

It is the business of pleasure that prevails—the labor of entertainment, the hard work of enjoyment.

The scenes are not monotonous. The eye meets rambling groups of men and women, dancing children, lads and maidens illustrating young love influenced by beer, brisk operations of athletic tendency on swings and ropes, and the busy effervescence of trade in shops and stalls. Sounds of tumbling tenpins, bullets tapping upon targets, hum of talk and laughing never diminish.

There are numberless "shooting galleries," not unlike those of the beer gardens, in which men give their minds with grave intensity to the discharge of penny popguns. There are little tents, in which pictorial shows are displayed, and wooden figures put through courses of mechanism. There are gymnastic appliances on which young men and women are invited to swing and hop, to tumble and seesaw, to wriggle on parallel bars, and to skim the air on edges of big wheels, revolving in somersaults and otherwise.

* * *

The day was cool, and the breezes from the forests and rivers were sweet and refreshing.

The Mayor was repeatedly cheered. . . .

For eighty-three years, this day of National Jubilee has been ushered in with the voices of cannon and of bells; and "bonfires and illuminations"—according to the pre-dictions of the great Statesmen— have everywhere attested a nation's pride and joy. Eighty-three years ago, the great truths of the Declaration were announced to the ages. And even though that announcement had been followed by the cross of disaster and defeat, though despotism had effaced its glowing lines in blood, and America had been today the hereditary footstool of some race of tyrants, there would still be occasion enough, though perchance not opportunity, for a celebration like this. . . .

119

There are wooden horses for timid infants to careen on, and live donkeys for the indulgence of more courageous youth. There are bowling alleys and billiard halls ever resounding with crash and click.

The "eighth wonder of the world," and conjurer of the nineteenth century, threatened to swallow a live tree, and to eat a sword by way of dessert; and of course the multitude rushed into the tent of the prodigy. Not least, if last recorded, there are countless and inexhaustible supplies of cheap refreshments, which never fail to find a ready market.

Here, beer reigns with supremest power. It drowns all other thoughts. Its flow is constant and unrestrained. Gurgling spigots emit steady streams. Tankards are tossed aloft with careless energy. Beside the river which sweeps by the woods, staid Germans stroll with mugs in hand. . . .

* * *

And shall it be forbidden us, my Countrymen, as we look back from the eminence of this day of glory over four-fifths of a century which has elapsed since our National birthday, to employ a language of exultation and thanksgiving over the way in which our God has led us?

And however it may be feared that the lessons of the Declaration of the Revolution have failed in their hold upon the most immediate recipients of their blessing, certain it is that their voice has gone out in all the earth, and has not yet ceased to vibrate in the heart of the natives. We are told that the very Arab has been heard to utter with reverence the name of Washington. . . .

Wagons roll in with full kegs and out with empty ones.

Toughs and ruffians, rowdies, loafers, shoulder hitters, and all sorts of tricksters—offering to bet you couldn't tell which thimble the little joker was under—roamed at large over the grounds. In one place was a sturdy German with a shooting gallery, offering two shots for 3¢ with an air gun. He was largely patronized and had his pockets loaded with 3¢ pieces.

Then there was a band of Negro minstrels whose broad hilarities drew an immense throng; and a surprising supply of fiddlers, each surrounded by a group of dancers. . . .

* * *

Far be it from me to ignore either the dangers or the sins of the Republic. I know how eternal must be that vigilance which is the price of liberty.

Has anyone yet claimed that liberty, once asserted in a fallen world, should thenceforth meet no obstacles? Have we not seen wave after wave, terror-created and full tide advanced, come threatening down upon us, only to break in harmless foam, and send their silent silvery reach far up the shore? . . .

Here in a small tent was a Spaniard, who did all sorts of tricks, throwing up knives, swallowing a sword, etc., at 10¢ a sight. . . .

* * *

And first and foremost, I think we should be aware of allowing the great cardinal principles of American liberty to fall into desuetude which precedes contempt. In the earlier life of these venerable men around me, the recurrence of this anniversary brought the Sabbath of the year. Then, in every town and hamlet in the land, gray-haired heroes whose personal sufferings and toils had engraven on their memory every incident of the War of Independence, listened with moistened eyes as the first principles of the gospel of liberty fell from the lips of the orator; and young men and boys stood by with hearts on fire to emulate the martyrdom of their fathers; and woman was there, both the matron and the maid, to hallow with her sympathy and inspire with her approval, the cause of human rights. . . .

In a large building on the grounds, known as Jones' Woods Hotel, were crowds of people taking dinner. There was a brass band on the balcony which played waltzes and quadrilles. Manners were at a discount, the knife and fork were thrown aside, and "all hands" were busy. The women did not hesitate taking the leg or wing of a chicken in their fingers, and short work was made of them.

At intervals, fights were extemporized, but the knockdowns did not amount to much. Late in the afternoon, a young rowdy, rejoicing in being connected with a gang called the "Hounds," was walking toward the outer gate, with a little wire basket of flowers, when another rowdy of the "Side Pockets" order met him and said, "Let's smell of dem flowers." Hound handed the basket to a companion and sticking his fist in Side Pocket's nose, said, "Smell ob dat." Both now went at it with a will, and punished each other considerably. Hound got the worst of it, and the last our reporter saw of him was heels and coatskirts among trees. . . .

And still, when we, who now stand in the meridian, were boys, the fire continued to burn; here and there a straggling relic of the Revolution could be hunted up to grace a platform on Independence Day, and we children looked on him with reverential awe and believed in him and his course religiously. But now, alas! The last of the Fathers has gone to his reward. . . .

The greatest attraction of all the rest, which superinduced this great rush of citizens to the Woods, was the announcement that the balloon *Louisa* would be inflated by 4 o'clock, and that Professor J. Pusey, the celebrated aeronautic hero of forty-eight flights, would ascend upon another voyage. Toward afternoon, as the hour approached for the ascent, there could not have been less than 10,- to 12,000 persons on the grounds.

At one end of an enclosure formed of ropes was the balloon, about half filled with gas, detained on terra firma by sandbags. At the other, were the preparations for manufacturing gas. Outside of the ropes was an immense crowd of men and women, and every available spot for sitting or standing was seized upon. . . .

And foolish men have babbled on the sacred theme; and the American eagle has been spread over the dreary continent on nonsense; and the star-spangled banner has been wrought into many a coat of motley, but still we return to our charge. This gospel is eternal; these principles must never be forgotten; we cannot afford to forget them. Why are they not taught in school? . . .

The slow and tedious process of inflation began at 9 o'clock in the morning. At one time, inflation appeared to be going on very fairly and several false alarms were got up which sent thousands flying in all directions to see the Professor off. But these were all the worse for frequent repetitions.

An awkward occurrence in the day's eventful history attracted some attention. At the hour of 4 o'clock —the time for the ascension—a small constable attended by one or more ex-constables, appeared on the grounds and asked Mr. Lingard to pay the amount of a judgment obtained against the late owner of the balloon (this is the same one that was picked up 40 miles at sea a short time ago; it weighs 170 pounds, is made of fine linen, varnished over with a dark brown color, is 60 feet high by 30 feet in diameter, and is capable of holding 1,500 cubic feet of gas). Mr. Lingard refused. Constable said he would have to make a levy. Mr. Lingard said, "There's the balloon, and it's my property. I have bought it and paid for it, and have shown you the receipts—now, if you think you are right, go ahead. . . ."

My Countrymen, let us guard the purity of the ballot box. Let us cultivate this faith in the virtue of the people—this charity to each other's political honesty. Let us cling to our system of popular education. . . .

Constable said he didn't want to make any disturbance. Mr. Lingard said he didn't want any trouble. He didn't know anything about the matter, but remarked particularly to the constable, "There's the balloon, and if you are going to make a levy, do it before we manufacture any more gas, and if you ain't, get out of the ropes. You're in the way." Constable said he would let the matter go, even if he burned his fingers, and left with his posse.

Professor Pusey was, however, in no better position after he got rid of the sheriff's officer than he was before. At 4 o'clock and even up to 6 o'clock, it was not more than half full of gas, and sensible people gave up all hopes of seeing it ascend at all that evening. Cries of, "Hurry up that balloon," and, "It's all humbug," etc., began to be freely used; and the crowd pressed thicker than ever around the enclosure, stirring up the professor to get up his balloon. The professor was somewhat excited by these noisy demonstrations and declared that though he had been up forty-eight times from different places, he was never so annoyed before. This was considered lame; forty-eight times were nothing; they wanted him to go up now.

At seven o'clock when there was scarcely anyone who was not ready to boil over with indignation, it was announced that the ascension would not be made. Loud cries were made for Professor Pusey but he did not appear. He had, it seems, taken his flight terrestrially. The disappointment of the people now showed itself in ill-tempered remarks. Professor Grant made a speech and described his mode of making gas. He said he had made enough to fill the balloon, but some evil disposed persons had pricked the cloth, thereby allowing the gas to escape. This subterfuge, of course, produced nothing but a laugh of derision.

A row was threatened. Loud cries of, "Cut the d——d balloon!" "Burn it!" "Tear it!" "Humbug!" etc., were raised. Many vowed vengeance on the professor—if they could only catch him.

The police found great trouble in getting the half-filled monster into their possession in safety. This was ultimately done, and the gas having been discharged, the balloon was locked up in the attic of the Hotel.

As there was no longer any hope of getting the ascent that evening, the crowds of people began to disperse about the grounds in different ways. Long lines of men, women, and children who wanted to see the sights in the city streamed down the walks, meeting at the entrance and crowding the cars which ran every few minutes and were crammed for hours. A fine band was in attendance and dancing was kept up upon a large platform which was lighted in the evening. It was a late hour of the night before the grounds were cleared.

Unknown Aeronauts   With his hand upon the catch, the aeronaut looks up at the sky. If it be partially cloudy, he watches till he is midway between the cloud that has passed and that which is coming, so that he may have a clear sky, and at least see the earth beneath; for the cloud which preceded will always precede, and that which follows will always follow.

* * *

No matter how agitated the balloon before its departure, no matter how violent the circumstances under which the ascent is effected, the moment the last hold upon the solid earth is cast off, all is perfect repose and stillness the most profound. The creaking of the car, the rustling of the silk, the heavy lurching of the distended sphere swayed to and fro by the breeze, shifting its load with sudden and energetic motion despite the efforts of the individuals who are struggling to retain it, all have ceased in an instant, and are succeeded by a degree of upright tranquility so intense as for a moment to absorb all other considerations, and almost confuse the mind of the voyager from the suddenness of the change, and its apparent incompatibility with the nature of the enterprise in which he is embarked.

* * *

As you ascend, the horizon goes up with you, level with the eye. The earth appears to be concave; hence its saucer-like appearance from a high altitude and not that convexity which would seem to be the right appearance of a globe.

* * *

There, projected upon a plane at right angles to the line of vision, the whole surface of the earth lies stretched beneath him. Distances which he was used to regard as important, contracted to a span; objects once imposing to him from their dimensions, *dwindled into insignificance. The whole face of nature, in fact, appears to have undergone a process of general equalization; the houses and trees, the mountains and the very clouds by which they are capped, have long since been consigned to one level; all of the natural irregularities of its surface completely obliterated, and the character of the* model *entirely superseded by that of the* plan. . . .

* * *

. . . rotating and counterrotating in a series of spiral curves as the balloon ascends from one air current to another, similar to that contact which a ship experiences when sailing through a bay and coming suddenly across a current dashing down from a river; a difficulty which presents itself in all these experiments, and varies the view incessantly. The use of a guide rope almost if not entirely destroys this tendency.

* * *

When the machine sails a considerable length of time at a great altitude and in a steady horizontal direction, it revolves in a pulsatory circulation, like the notched wheel in a clock which is actuated by the pendulum . . .

. . . as a similar-shaped vessel with a string fastened to its upper axis and suspended from the ceiling of a room . . .

. . . how very slight must be the wave of atmosphere to put it in motion, poised as it is in either case, upon its center of gravity . . .

I have reversed the motion by simply using a palm-leaf fan . . .

* * *

The extraordinary silence. Here and only here, can absolute silence be said to have any existence at all, save for the friendly occasional creak of a rope or the basket as one of the crew changes position.

On earth we have nothing to compare with the awful stillness of these eerie solitudes. Some noise—be it the sighing of the wind, the pattering of the rain, the fall of a crumbling particle of rock—will break the tranquility of the veil, the loneliest wilderness, the loftiest peak. But here nature appears to be voiceless.

But here, too are none of those delightful sounds which maintain the idea of animation even in the veriest desert; none of those fragrant exhalations by which every tree and flower gives vent to its own particular sentiments.

* * *

Fifteen hundred feet up, silence is broken occasionally by the barking of a dog heard very faintly, or by the sound of a voice hailing the balloon.

* * *

At 2,600 feet, during the silence of the night, the slight noises made by the crickets are heard very plainly; at 2,950 feet the croaking of frogs is plaintively distinct. At 3,300 feet, the current of a stream, at all rapid, produces the same effect as the rush of the cascades. At 3,900 feet the rumble of vehicles upon the pavement is audible; at 4,500 feet the beating of a drum and the sound of a band. The shouts of people are sometimes audible at 5,000 feet, as also the crowing of a cock or the tolling of a bell; the bark of a dog at 6,000—the report of a gun attains the same height; the noise of a train at 8,200 . . .

At 8,940 feet they let off a violet bee, which flew away swiftly, making a humming noise.

The whistle of a steam engine may be heard at ten thousand feet . . .

At 11,000 feet they liberated a green linnet, which flew away directly, but soon returned and settled on the stays of the balloon. Then, it took a second flight, and dashed downwards to the earth, describing a tortuous yet almost perpendicular track.

A pigeon, placed on the edge of the car, rested awhile; now launched into the abyss, it fluttered irregularly and seemed at first to try its wings on the thin element, till after a few strokes, it gained more confidence and, whirling in large circles or spirals, like the birds of prey, it precipitated itself towards the mass of extended clouds where it was lost from sight.

* * *

As the aeronaut looks out from his airy domicile upon the immense void . . .

For the first time in his life he is really, and feels, alone—a single inhabitant in the great ethereal ocean of the universe.

To the production of these sensations, no other situation is at all competent. It is more than grandeur. The mind appears to expand itself commensurately with the magnitude of the scene that surrounds it.

* * *

Contemplating a bottle in the act of falling from the car, while at a superior elevation, the complete isolation of the beholder, the apparent infirmity of the fragile vehicle over the side of which he peers with impunity; the sudden force with which the bottle appears to escape from his hand, frequently enhanced by the occurrence at the same time of a similar motion in a contrary direction on the part of the balloon, tracing with the eyes its progress as it descends toward the earth; the equally sudden retardation which, after it has dropped a few feet, it seems to have experienced, together with the length of time it afterwards remains in sight, and the comparative slowness of the changes that increasing distances operate in its dimensions—the silent magnificence of the abyss into which it plunges . . .

Then I threw a new bread basket from the car. It had not gone far before it assumed a rapid rotary motion, bottom downwards, its upper being the concave side, looking like a beautiful rosette, set into a circular motion on its center . . .

Throwing down other substances of different kinds and shapes, I observed that they all fell with the same counterclockwise rotary motion.

* * *

Of all the sounds, however, which meet the ear of the adventurer in these exalted regions, none appears to bear so impressive a character, or to be productive of such awful sensations as that occasioned by the snapping of the valve in the upper part of the balloon, when in the act of closing after some occasional discharge of gas in the course of the excursion. The sudden sharpness which it displays in common with the rest, the unusual direction from which it issues—a direction from whence no sound is naturally expected to proceed, the intimate connection between it, the office it has to perform, and the fate of the aeronaut by whom it is worked, together with the drumlike intonation which instantly supervenes, caused by the extreme tension of the silken dome which in a manner serves like a sounding board, to sustain and prolong its fleeting impulses . . .

* * *

Scarcely has a sound been promulgated in ordinary situations than it is immediately encountered by a thousand obstacles that alter, impede, protract, derange, and qualify its vibrations, interfering with its simplicity. But in a balloon basket, deprived in a measure of all those artificial asperities by which it is usually distinguished, its character becomes totally altered. It strikes upon the senses in all its native purity: sharply, simply, strongly— never continuing beyond the natural duration of its own primary vibration.

Presently, it was all overcast below, the thunder rattling like small arms without any of the rolling reverberations that are heard underneath. Several times the surface of the lower stratum swelled up suddenly like a boiling cauldron, which was immediately followed by the most brilliant ebullition of sparkling coruscations. Twice it swelled up, or rather shot up, like an immense pyramid, which was also quickly followed by an evolution of promiscuous flashes—the zigzag coruscations of electricity looking like sparkling diamonds shooting athwart snowbanks—which then disappeared again, as though it had dissolved; the vessel all the while moving with a smooth, apparently motionless, but grand and majestic pace—twenty, forty, and not unfrequently eighty miles per hour.

It was a magnificent sight. . . .

*   *   *

Glancing upwards, the sky appears to be falling, as if the ceiling of the universe had given way; and yonder dark cloud which had seemed to be motionless is now tumbling headlong upon you and will, infallibly, crush the balloon like a moth. It requires some little consideration to correct this delusion and satisfy yourself that the change is in you and not in the world itself . . .

*   *   *

The novice in aerial navigation almost instinctively holds his breath and awaits the awful collision as he sees the distance narrow between his frail skiff and the frowning piles above; but they open as if by magic, and the balloon glides into their midst without a shock or tremor . . .

*   *   *

The clouds receive you, at first in a light gauze of vapor, and then in a chilly embrace. You are enveloped for a short time in a sort of obscurity, but there is nothing to fear; for there is not the slightest obstruction in these pathless expanses.

Shortly it becomes lighter, the light gradually increasing, till it is succeeded by a flood of light, at first striking, then dazzling; and you pass out of a dense cloud, to where the clouds open out into bold and fantastic shapes, showing you light and shade and spectral scenes, embellished with prismatic colors, disporting themselves around you in wild grandeur, till at length you break out into brilliant sunshine, and the clouds roll away into a perfect sea of vapor, closing like a trap door, and shutting you out from the dear old world where we all lead such a life of charmed misery.

The whole plane of vision was one extended ocean of foam, broken into a thousand fantastic forms; here swelling into mountains, then sinking into lengthened fosses, or exhibiting the appearance of vast whirlpools. Enormous clouds like gigantic castles, now at the fastness of Nature herself. Massive buttresses and ramparts seem to rear up from unseen hands, and so little wind is stirring that all this gorgeous pageantry is not fretted away before the changing breeze, but remains as though it were destined to endure forever. The delicate traceries of the cirri are still far above . . .

130

* * *

But did we say we were in absolute solitude? If so, imagine the startled look of an aeronaut on issuing from a cloud, as he sees before him at a distance of some 30 or 40 yards, the figure of another balloon! One remarkable feature, however, instantly attracts his attention. The car of the stranger is placed in the center of a huge disc, consisting of several concentric circles—the interior one being yellowish white, the next pale blue, the third yellow, followed by a ring of grayish red, and finally, by one of light violet. That car, too, is occupied. Its tenants are engaged in returning the scrutiny, and their attitudes express equal surprise. By and by, one of them lifts his hand; but that is just what one of the aeronauts has done. Another motion is made, and this is imitated to the letter. A laugh from the living voyageurs follows. They have discovered that the stranger is an optical apparition, for on examination, it is found to correspond with their own machine, line for line, rope for rope, and man for man; except that they, the living ones, are not surrounded by a glory as if they were resplendent saints.

This beautiful phenomenon is due to the reflection or refrac-

tion of light from the little vesicles of vapor, magnified or diminished by the aeronauts' relative distance from the clouds, and by their position in relation to the sun. It must not be confused with the ordinary shadow of the balloon, which, under fitting conditions and in a more or less elongated form, generally appears to accompany them like some spectral shark in pitiless pursuit of an infected ship.

* * *

*The most favorable arrangement, however, for the views of
the aeronaut who feels an interest and a gratification in the study
of the picturesque, is decidedly that in which the clouds, from
their broken and disconnected nature, spread at unequal intervals throughout the empty space of air, admit occasional glimpses
of the earth in different directions, and passing gradually over its
surface, in succession reveal an ever-varying prospect.*

* * *

*. . . twenty-five miles an hour is the mean rate at which a
body floating in atmosphere may be expected to be trans-
ported . . .*

* * *

*The blood begins to course more freely when up a mile or two
with a balloon—the excretory vessels are more freely opened—
the gastric juice pours into the stomach more rapidly—the liver,
kidneys, and heart work under expanded action—the brain re-
ceives and sends more exalted inspirations—the whole animal
and mental system becomes intensely quickened, and more of
the chronic morbid matter is exhaled and thrown off in an hour
or two of a fine summer's day than the invalid can get rid of in a
voyage from New York to Madeira, by sea.*

*The appetite is extraordinarily affected in a balloon ascension,
and this feature always gives a ravenous appetite for animal
food.*

* * *

*The problem to be solved is not exactly how you will skim the
surface of the water in a boat, but rather how you could drive a*

*frigate through the fluid with its sails set when sunk to a depth of
many feet; and this whole body of water in motion in a different
direction.*

*. . . entirely surrounded by and immersed in the fluid which
supports it, moving necessarily at the same rate as the current of
air in which it happens to be. . . .*

*Were it possible to tinge that portion of the atmosphere im-
mediately surrounding the balloon with color and commit her to
the discretion of the elements, she would—apart from all fluctuations in the level of her course—continue to bear the same
tinted medium along with her, even until she had completed her
course around the globe.*

*Sails were, of course, useless since there was no wind to fill
them, and for the same reason, there being no current, the rudder
had no action on the direction of motion.*

*Riggings, paddles, wings, fins, wheels, rudders, oars, helms,
sails, and counter sails will never be able to prevent the wind
from sweeping away the whole concern.*

*In dealing with a bottle of frisky porter or highly impatient
soda water, it may be well to act cautiously, lest the cork should
go like a shot through the envelope of the balloon; and in drinking the contents it would be wise to wait till effervescence has
subsided.*

*There are no busy police to watch your movements; and no
customhouse officer to search your car, and ask, "What have
you got in that bottle? . . ."*

*. . . but let me tell you, there is one setoff against these com-
forts. There are no inns; so that when what we had "got in that
bottle," which was some sherry, was exhausted in drinking to
the health of our friends, we could not get our bottle replenished
for love nor money. So you see, things are not absolutely perfect
even there. . . .*

TO THE EDITOR OF THE NEW YORK *Tribune: Sir:* In your paper of the 6th, I find my name mixed up with certain other parties in reference to the balloon failure in Jones' Woods on the 4th, imputing that failure to the imperfectness of my method of making hydrogen gas.

The gas was furnished by me and was sufficient both in quantity and quality, but certain mischievous spectators perforated the balloon with bullets and otherwise. No less than seven holes and one large rent were found in the silk through which the gas escaped.

The gas, therefore, passed out through these holes as rapidly as it was eliminated from the gas generators. This explains the reason why inflation of the balloon did not progress after 2 o'clock, although the gas was generating after that hour with equal rapidity.

In view of the whole question, Mr. Editor, permit me to remark that in the failure of the balloon ascension, Mr. Pusey was in no degree delinquent. Blame ought to be imputed only to those who chose to make a target of the balloon.

For myself, I have only to say that I worked with all the energy in my physical and intellectual being, as all on the ground can attest, for the purpose of gratifying the public, and assisting a stranger; and evolving a beautiful and scientific public display, in which I had no pecuniary interest whatsoever other than the reimbursement of my outlays.

The assumption that my plan of making hydrogen gas did not work well, may be put down for what it is worth. My business is manufacturing and displaying the Calcium Light, requiring as a daily business, the production of hydrogen gas through the most economical and scientific means.

In conclusion, Mr. Editor, I will only say that my whole life has been used with the intent to benefit my fellow men, not to disappoint or mislead them.

Robert Grant

CHAPTER 8

Messrs. Wise, La Mountain, and Gager become involved in lengthy and scolding correspondence about themselves and their recent flight . . . But more important, perhaps, the jettisoned Express bag is rescued.

The idea of sailing in the atmosphere is at all events of very great antiquity; but old as it is, it has never got beyond the condition of an idea, and in all human probability never will. Still it must be admitted that the latest experiment in aerostation has been more successful than any of the preceding ones of which we have any record. Two well-known and experienced aeronauts— Messrs. Wise and La Mountain— have reasoned themselves into the conviction that to cross the Atlantic by balloon is by no means infeasible and having determined to give some evidence toward upholding that conviction, started from the city of St. Louis last Friday evening, on an experimental trip to the Atlantic coast.

The chief point of distinction between this and previous air voyages consists of the fact that the place of landing was indicated on the program, though deviated from pretty considerably in the execution of the project. No plan has yet been discovered by which a balloon can be guided in a course contrary to the direction of the wind. But Mr. La Mountain has made observations with respect to wind currents which lead him to the conclusion that at a certain elevation from the earth, and more particularly in the summer season, the direction of the wind is almost uniform from west to east. Of this knowledge he proposed to take advantage, and to the ordinary modes of elevating or depressing the balloon so as to get into the desired current, he added an invention of his own in the shape of rotary fans.

If, therefore, the theory about the wind currents were correct, and if the contingency of storms could be guarded against, there might really be some ground for faith in the ultimate success of aerial navigation. But the winds are not to be relied upon, and storms are dangerously frequent during the summer season, so we find that Messrs. Wise and La Mountain, instead of landing near the Atlantic Coast as they proposed, came down in the northwestern part of New York, four or five hundred miles from this city; and that, owing to a hurricane which struck them as they descended, it is little short of a miracle that they were not dashed to pieces in that fearful passage through the woods.

Therefore, while this last experiment in ballooning is the most successful that has been yet made, it does not hold out the faintest shadow of encouragement to those who believe that this mode of traveling across the Atlantic will ultimately be inaugurated. On the contrary, it only furnishes another proof to the many which previous experiences have furnished of the utter impossibility of such a thing. When we see how powerless against storms are even those birds that are strongest and best adapted to resist them, how sea birds are blown into land, and land birds blown out to sea, we may rest assured that no flying machine, the work of mere human invention, can ever be practically utilized for traveling purposes. All such attempts must result, as they heretofore have, in failure, sometimes ludicrous and sometimes deplorable.

TO THE EDITOR OF THE NEW YORK *Tribune: Sir:* It seems to me that a little explanation of what I have contended for twenty years seems now in place.

I say there is a current of air blowing from west to east continually, and this current runs never less than fifty miles an hour; oftener sixty, seventy, and eighty. As we ascend higher in the current, it runs faster, until we find it changing a little south of east. The lower current, near the earth, runs to the north of east. I have found these currents at all times of the year from the 1st of April to the 12th of December. From my experiences of finding them thirty-six times out of forty trials, I contend that regular and precise voyages can be made from the west to the east. Why, then, it is asked, did we not sail to the city of New York and deliver our Express bag? It is a very rational inquiry and deserves a rational explanation.

It could and should have been done. The reason why it was not done is this: Some of our party did not provide themselves with extra clothing. Immediately after leaving St. Louis, I took the balloon to an altitude at which she was making due east. In this current we sailed until some of my companions shivered with the cold, so that the balloon quivered. Mr. La Mountain had taken no extra clothing, and the other two were not fully provided for the change of temperature. I had on two undershirts, woolen drawers, cloth coat, Cassimere pants, and over these I had two woolen blankets; but the expostulations of my companions to come down into a more congenial temperature could not be unheeded. I admonished them, however, of our advertisement to sail for New York; but in response was told that if we got into the State, the program would be fulfilled. I also told them that the lower current would take us on the lakes, as it was coming from the southwest; but to this it was answered that we could cross the lakes if we had ballast enough when we got to them.

We finally agreed upon that plan, and to make the voyage one of distance and experiments. One experiment was to try and sail near the earth or water. We did sail 170 miles down over Lake Erie, and at no time over 600 feet above the water. This showed that balloons have no greater tendency to water than to land. Many aeronauts have stated that balloons will not keep up over water.

You refer to my silence as to the propelling machinery. *That* I had not devised nor recommended, and I had no faith in its efficiency from the beginning, as Mr. Gager and La Mountain well know. They never made an attempt to try it out. It was thought to endanger the balloon while hitching on the car and boat and thus remained ungeared. I well knew then that they would not attempt to screw on the fans when we were aloft, unless they would incur a danger as great as that incurred by Thurston, when he attempted an unsuccessful feat in straddling his valve plate. Propellers upon the ordinary rigged balloon will do no good, for this reason: the car or platform upon which the propellers are to be worked is not substantially fixed to the balloon. Hanging by ropes from the balloon, it only serves to wobble it about, and at best, to give it a rotary and gyrating motion. I tried it 14 years ago. With an equatorial hoop around the balloon, with wooden braces to the car which would give it stability and unity, something may be done with propellers and rudder. You will thus see that I have not failed on that point.

My purpose was simply to make a long voyage from west to east, and in that voyage learn what may be done systematically with balloons. I am now convinced that we can go from St. Louis to Baltimore, Philadelphia, and New York City with system and precision. I hold, and am ready to demonstrate—as soon as I can raise $6,000—that we can sail from New York City to Great Britain with system and precision. This we can do with our present knowledge of ballooning. All I ask is a fair chance—a little more experience—one, two, or three more transcontinental trips. We were caught in a terrific gale just when we were landing west of Rochester, for the purpose of sending the U.S. Company's Express to your city and delivering it in less time than they ever delivered one before. But for that accidental gale, we would have fulfilled the promise.

Respectfully yours,
John Wise

TO THE EDITOR OF THE NEW YORK *Tribune: Sir:* In your journal of Saturday, you published a letter from John Wise. It is due to my reputation that its covert insinuations against me should be answered.

Mr. Wise was not a partner in the enterprise. The St. Louis *Herald* of July 2nd, reports this from his speech just before the ascension: "Mr. Wise stated that he merely went with the adventurers on invitation as an old campaigner." This was so. An effort was made to induce me to admit him to copartnership. For several reasons, I declined.

Mr. Wise, of course, cannot claim to be the author of a theory on winds, original in its present shape with Lt. Maury.

Mr. Wise says that we could have reached New York had I not neglected to provide myself with extra clothing! I beg his pardon. Had he been less sleepy and more observant during the trip, he would have made no such statement. There were several reasons for the failure. 1) Mr. Wise fell asleep with a tense valve rope in his hand and the nap cost us 5,000 feet of gas. 2) During the entire night both upper and lower currents were blowing northeast, and carrying us at an angle toward Nova Scotia; though twice, on awakening and rubbing his eyes, Mr. Wise insisted we were going southwest. 3) During most of the forenoon, the local and upper currents were east. 4) We had too many passengers. 5) The tornado we encountered was blowing northeast, and we could not rid ourselves of extra ballast to escape it. I did not once descend from any altitude on account of cold; and Mr. Wise knows it. Mr. Wise did not once "remind" us of our promises to reach New York, and he knows it. He was, it is true, "warmly clothed." I have never yet needed such precaution.

Mr. Wise said he did not devise or recommend propellers. I have letters from him in which he does endorse and recommend my plans. The editor of the Troy *Times* reports: "Mr. Wise pronounces the machinery perfect and admirable in every respect." He wrote in a letter to a Lancaster editor that, "the propellers sent their boat through the water at six miles an hour and are just the thing." Mr. Wise says the propeller machinery was left "because it was thought to endanger the balloon." It was left because, just before starting, several screws and bolts were found to have been broken, and none of us wished to stop for repairs. No one ever thought of screwing on the fans when aloft.

Mr. Wise says the car hanging by ropes will only "wobble about and give the balloon a rotary or gyrating motion." Two hundred and thirty-nine ascensions should have taught him that it is only on passing from one current to another that the car can be affected by causes that do not likewise affect the globe. The machinery and its arrangements were correct.

I did not promise to reach New York City. Mr. Wise made that promise and I objected. I did tell the people that we would reach the Atlantic; and so we should have, but for the gale which was not "accidental," as Mr. Wise says, but providential. We were not descending to send the mail back to New York but to land two of our passengers. Mr. Wise cannot cross the ocean in accordance with his plan for less than $20,000. He told me no consideration would induce him to attempt to make the passage unless the balloon cable was capable of elevating 20 tons, enabling him to carry a pilot boat.

From first to last, I have been robbed of just credit, slandered, ridiculed, and placed in a false position by this man, whom I allowed to accompany me. He has conveyed everywhere the idea that I was a fellow of some pluck, but having no scientific knowledge of ballooning, and that his wisdom barely compensated for my blunders. I go to Watertown today for the wreck of my balloon, which will at once be rebuilt. In October, I shall cross the Atlantic. If, meanwhile, Mr. Wise considers the matter of sufficient importance to test our relative capacities—scientifically considered in a trial trip from San Francisco to the Atlantic seaboard with balloons of equal size—he knows my address.

John La Mountain

142

We desire to take no part in this not very pleasing or profitable controversy, but we are authorized by Mr. Gager to state that Mr. La Mountain is mistaken in some of the above statements. Instead of Mr. Wise being a mere passenger on the recent voyage, he was, according to Mr. Gager, a partner, owning the same share in the balloon as Mr. La Mountain, namely, one quarter; and this share he still owns, while Mr. La Mountain owns no more.

TO THE EDITOR OF THE NEW YORK *Tribune: Sir:* I think, with Mr. Gager, that we ought to have no controversy about this matter, but be thankful that our lives were saved. We are thus enabled to communicate to our fellowmen the results of our experience. I desire to extract glory in this eventful experiment from no persons; my whole aim is to promote the art of aerial navigation, and with it the science of meteorology.

If Mr. La Mountain feels himself wronged by my being a partner in the balloon and having, by a written contract, the "chief Directorship" of it, I will only say that he can buy me out in cash at what I have invested in it.

Mr. Gager is the projector of the whole thing, so far as the Balloon *Atlantic* is concerned, and with him as his partner, I have and hold the contract—not La Mountain. I herewith submit one of a great number of letters I received from Mr. La Mountain on the subject of the balloon *Atlantic*. He is an aeronaut of one year's practice, and I furnished him his balloon, *Pride of America,* with which he made a number of ascensions, and in which he took up Mr. Gager at Bennington, Vermont.

Without consulting Mr. Gager on what I state here, I pledge you my word that he will vouch for its accuracy. I will trouble you or your readers no more with anything that Mr. La Mountain or his friends may say about me, believing that time and truth will correct all things.

Respectfully yours,
John Wise

John Wise—Dear Sir:

I can never sufficiently express my thanks to you for your kind advice to me, which has been the cause of my past success; and I must look to you for more. I want to see you in New York City because I want to show you some things there which will pay you well for coming to the city. You will have a chance of seeing the motive power and all about the rubber and so on. As I told you before, you shall have the job of making my balloon, for I know you can do it better than I. In this letter I send you a sample of rubber-coated silk. We can give this silk a coat of oil; in that way it would, I think, hold the gas almost forever. I told Mr. Gager about you, and he said he would be very glad to have you have a hand in the balloon, if you wish, and use your name. I do not think I will try to cross the Atlantic next summer, but I hope we can make money enough then to build the *Atlantic*.

Please write to me soon. I am, dear Sir,

Yours truly,

Lansingburg, Jan. 16, 1859   John La Mountain

TO THE EDITOR OF THE NEW YORK *Tribune: Sir:* Having noticed the many articles published in various journals in reference to the late aerial voyage from St. Louis, many of which are incorrect and do much injustice to the several parties, I would respectfully ask you to make some corrections.

An account was published in the Troy *Times* and copied into your own and other papers as my account, and in *Frank Leslie's Illustrated* as an "Account of the Voyage in My Own Words." That account was not written by me, and it does Mr. Wise much injustice as it represents him as using language which he did not use; and many other decorations which are therein contained are far from being "my own words." The account was first published in the Troy *Times* and gleaned by their reporter from about ten minutes' conversation with me and the account of Mr. Wise as published in the Albany *Journal*. The *Times* did me the favor in their next edition to say that "it was not, as many supposed, written by me"; but as it had been so extensively copied into various journals, I feel that justice to all parties interested demands of me this explanation. It has also been stated that I furnished the capital for the enterprise, and that the ride cost me $2,000. Both statements are far from correct. The capital for building this airship was furnished by five persons. Although the balloon was wrecked in her descent to the earth, she can be made as good as when she started upon the voyage for a sum not exceeding $200.

The interest of the public in this great enterprise seems to me to demand of us who were intimately connected in carrying it out, a correct statement of its whole history, from its first inception to the termination of our voyage, given to the public over the signatures of Mr. Wise, Mr. La Mountain, and me, at as early a day as practicable.

I have not seen either of these gentlemen since we parted for our several homes. I truly hope each one of the parties may be actuated only by such motive as shall lead but to the advancement of so noble a science and art.

Truly yours,
O. M. Gager

The art of navigating the air has reached, in our day and country, a very high degree of advancement. The vigorous and successful achievements of the distinguished aeronauts, now rapidly pushing forward their experiments in the United States, bid fair to afford a favorable solution to the problem of adapting balloons to practical use as traveling vehicles. The late ascension of Mr. Wise and his companion goes far in demonstrating their capabilities to answer the purpose to which this daring and skillful operator is seeking to apply them. That astonishing excursion marks a new era in aerostatic history; and although the particular end for which it was undertaken was not fully accomplished, yet enough was gained to encourage the most sanguine hope that further trials will lead to more propitious results. The art is evidently approaching a degree of perfection which will give it an enlarged claim to public favor and confidence. Even skepticism itself will grow gradually feebler. When a method shall be devised for accurate and steady steerage, aided by a more perfect power of ascending and descending, the balloon will career through the empyrean expanse with as much ease and safety as a stately vessel speeds through the ocean.

OSWEGO, WEDNESDAY, JULY 6TH. The Express bag, sent by the U.S. Express Agent, in the balloon *Atlantic*, was picked up yesterday in the lake. Contains over forty letters—one enclosing a $1,000 draft on a New York bank.

It had its address and history written upon it, so that, when found, it was promptly forwarded.

TO THE EDITOR OF THE NEW YORK *Tribune: Sir:* Balloons can be built of capacities sufficient to carry several tons of weight. The conveyance of letters, passengers, and gold will soon become a profitable business. A few voyages will bring larger experience and lessen the dangers which, if we may judge from the number of times experienced aeronauts have returned in safety from the regions above, are greatly exaggerated. But dangers or no dangers, demonstrate the possibility of the thing, and the love of gain will do the rest. When aerial journeys from San Francisco and New York have become an old story, and not until then, will it be time to think of a voyage across the Atlantic.

T.C.P.

O. A. GAGER

Friend Wise:

Dear Sir:

I have not yet seen John La Mountain since we left him in Adams. You have doubtless seen what reports to be "his account" written by Mr. Demers of the Troy Times. Also an account of his reception on his return to Lansingburg. The motives that have prompted all the articles in the Troy Times are plainly seen and generally known by Mr. La Mountain's friends; and I am confident the general feeling of the sensible public is much changed since their publication. I was asked while in Troy by Mr. Demers how I liked Mr. La Mountain's account. My reply was that I thought it was unworthy of notice, knowing that it was written by himself (Demers). I could only say that I thought it rather ungenerous for Mr. La Mountain to allow his signature to be affixed to an article stating "he was deserted by his fellows, sick and disabled," when he turned back of his own accord; and at the time when I divided with him all the funds I had with me, being enough to have brought him safely home.

I am, as ever,

Truly yours,

O A Gager

TO THE EDITORS OF *Harper's Weekly:* Your own journal, as well as many other respectable papers, have been imposed on by fabricated accounts, purporting to be from Mr. O. A. Gager and from Mr. John La Mountain.

Permit me to say I have no ill feeling against Mr. La Mountain. I verily believe that no trouble would have arisen with him had he not placed himself in the hands of an indiscreet relation connected with the Troy *Times.* This person is attempting to build up a reputation for Mr. La Mountain by destroying mine, which I have been more than 20 years in acquiring. Time will show with what success. As for me, my business is to sail balloons, to improve the system of aerial navigation, to teach it to others, to improve the art in every way I can, and not to engage in controversies over this or that experiment. I claim to have done nothing but an ordinary duty in our late trip—just what any other man of the same experience and inclinations might have done.

We all felt devoted to our mission, sincere and harmonious in our action, until a gentleman of the Troy *Times* thought fit to mar that harmony by his ill-directed and ill-timed intermeddling.

Respectfully yours,
John Wise

CHAPTER 9

How promiscuous should one be in lightening a balloon by raining ballast down upon the hapless populace? . . . La Mountain learns of Prof. T. S. C. Lowe's intention to cross the Atlantic Ocean . . . Lowe must not be first; so La Mountain immediately begins practice flights, the second of which ends in almost total disaster.

WATERTOWN, NEW YORK: JULY 4TH. Mr. La Mountain arrived here this morning with the balloon, and announces that as soon as the balloon is repaired, he will make another voyage from Chicago eastward.

There is one feature of balloon sailing which threatens to assume very practical importance, if the art is to pass into the category of ordinary human occupations. We mean the system of lightening balloons by "heaving over" ballast in a promiscuous manner upon the earth below. It is impossible to read without a certain discomposure Mr. La Moun-

tain's exciting account of the means he adapted for relieving his ship when he had lost her buoyancy in the storm. The *Atlantic* took up seven hundred pounds of ballast, and a miscellaneous supply of iron fans, post, bars, carpetbags, and other baggage more or less weighty. She came down *minus* her entire cargo. It happened that in this case the good vessel was unloaded chiefly into the lake, though Mr. La Mountain does admit that he once heard his sandbags strike with a "thud" upon the roof of a house.

Suppose that house was on the shore, and the reader seated there, enjoying his evening cigar and a distant view of the changing sea. Or suppose a pair of lovers rowing in a boat upon the summer waters of some rural Como, "youth on the prow and pleasure at the helm," and the same suddenly saluted by three carpetbags and a twenty-pound crowbar falling from the skies. The fate of Aeschylus was romantic certainly, and though it would be more honorable to be killed by a sandbag in the cause of science than to have one's crown cracked by a tortoise dropped from the talons of an eagle, the net result to the earth-creeping man would be the same in both cases.

Will Messrs. Wise and La Mountain be good enough to take this matter into consideration?

Unknown *Aeronaut*

Meanwhile, on the cars bound west, Mr. La Mountain purchased a New York paper, in which he found an article giving an elaborate description of the mammoth balloon being built by T. S. Carlincourt Lowe at Hoboken, for the Atlantic voyage. With that rapidity of determination which characterizes him, he got off the cars at Rome—although ticketed some distance further—took the next train of cars east, connected with the Hudson River train at Troy, and went on to New York without stopping to see a single friend.

Arriving at Jersey City, he found matters so secretly conducted there that he could not obtain sight of the monster balloon. Going back to New York he traced out the author of the article, and obtained an introduction to him under an assumed name, representing himself as a mechanic who had devoted much attention to the study of ballooning, and who was desirous to make a passage with Lowe if he could persuade himself that the arrangements had been properly made. Mr. La Mountain learned that the monster balloon was almost completed, and its owner would certainly attempt the passage. He then went to Mr. Oatman, who had pledged him $20,000 to build an Atlantic balloon, informed him of what he had learned and proposed to go right to work if the funds were furnished, build his balloon in less than two weeks and make his trip ahead of Lowe. Mr. Oatman objected, said there was no use of entering a field already occupied; and told him that if the big balloon failed, he would then furnish the funds, not before.

Mr. La Mountain returned to Troy greatly excited. It was his opinion that Mr. Oatman had abandoned him. He believed that Mr. Gager had induced Oatman to help Lowe for the purpose of ruining him. He felt he was about to be deprived of all he had labored, studied, and sacrificed time and money to accomplish just when the object was within his reach. He came to us, and had long and absorbing conversation. Lowe, he said, was advertised to leave on the fifth of October and, if he started under favorable circumstances, was sure to accomplish the voyage which

152

he said, "would be the end of John La Mountain." Then, reflecting upon the subject a moment, he declared that rather than have Lowe cross the ocean first, he would make the attempt with his small balloon.

The conclusion Mr. La Mountain reached was that the easterly current found four miles above the earth would carry him at least sixty miles an hour; that therefore the passage could be accomplished in less than two days; that a hundred pounds of ballast would be all he should need.

Stating a time when the eastern current is less to be depended upon than at other periods, he said, "Lowe has never studied this matter, and he would be fool enough to start just at that time. Never mind—let them all desert me. I will fill the balloon with pure hydrogen in some back yard and go over before Lowe, anyway. We will show them who was the originator of Atlantic ballooning." And on bidding us goodbye, he added, "Don't fear for me. It will be all right, sooner than some people imagine."

Before proceeding to Watertown, Mr. La Mountain went to Lansingburg, where his wife was then stopping.

Mr. T. S. Carlincourt Lowe, an aeronaut of six years' practical experience and a mechanic of common ingenuity, has been for several months engaged in building and perfecting an airship of unparalleled dimensions, with which he proposes to undertake the transit of the Atlantic Ocean. This daring scheme has been the pet ambition of many aeronauts, who have lacked either the boldness to carry out their plans or have not had the pecuniary means to build the proper machinery. Mr. Lowe has invested some $22,000 in the construction of a machine with which he is confident he can make air voyages of days' or weeks' duration. He began his work some eight months ago; but hearing that his friend Mr. John Wise, had in contemplation the construction of a machine for the transatlantic trip, Mr. Lowe laid aside his work for six months. Mr. Wise having given up building his machine, Mr. Lowe resumed work on his invention, and for the past two months the labor of persons— as many as sixty—has been constant. But two or three weeks more is required to put the machine in working order, ready for the great experiment.

La Mountain   *Mary, I have been thinking and talking the matter over, and I'm going across the ocean with my small balloon. They have secretly built a big balloon in New York, to head me off on the Atlantic voyage, but I am going to show the people of this country a trick that they don't dream of now. Lowe shan't have the credit for my discoveries. If, after my one ascension, you shouldn't hear from me, make up your mind that I've landed in Europe. . . .*

The chief difficulty in crossing the ocean in a balloon arises from the gradual exhaustion of its buoyant power. (Scarcely a moment passes without some call for the aeronaut's interposition, either to check the balloon by the relection of ballast, or to control its ascent by the proportionate discharge of gas; a process by which, it is unnecessary to observe, the whole power of the balloon, however great its dimensions, must in time be exhausted, and sooner or later terminate its career by succumbing to the laws of terrestrial gravitation.) No balloon in existence, it is supposed, could retain its buoyancy for more than two or three days— too short a time, of course, to attempt a voyage of three thousand miles. But as the buoyant power is in exact proportion to the gas enclosed in the balloon, it would seem to follow that by increasing the latter, the former would be multiplied; in other words the larger the balloon the longer it will float in the air. Acting on this theory, Mr. Lowe has built a balloon considerably larger than the largest ever built hitherto.

AT THE APPROACH of night, or upon the passage through clouds charged with vapor, or under the influence of a shower of rain, the gas becomes contracted by loss of heat; a large quantity of moisture becomes absorbed by the balloon netting and other apparatus, frequently to the extent of two or three hundred weight, requiring an immediate discharge of ballast to that amount to prevent her being borne to the ground.

As the morning approaches, moisture becomes dissipated; expansion is caused by the sun's shining on the balloon, and, there being no means of recovering the discharged ballast, the lightened balloon rapidly rises in the air, her contents expanding again in her course, rendering its liberation necessary to prevent bursting. . . .

He has provided two large buoys. These are to be filled with condensed gas, which can be projected into the balloon by means of a force pump, to compensate for any loss of gas by leakage; and will pump gas from the balloon into the condensers as well. The gas which is forced into the balloon from the condensers, immediately expanding, adds much to the ascending power. To descend, the abstraction of a certain quantity of gas from the balloon reduces this ascending power, and when compressed into the condensers, acts as ballast. This is very beautiful in theory, but it yet remains for Mr. Lowe to determine by actual experiment whether the practical working will be equally admirable.

TO THE EDITOR OF THE NEW YORK *Tribune: Sir:* In your report of Mr. Lowe's aerial machinery this morning, my name is used in connection with the account in a manner as to do me a serious injury if not corrected. The account says I have abandoned the project of constructing my transatlantic balloon. My present sojourn in this city, however, is an account of that very business. I have ordered seven thousand yards of stout Suchan pongee silk from Europe, for the construction of my airship.

I have never for a moment abandoned that project. My late experiments in the eastern current were specifically made with the view of aiding me in its simplification. And I am sure I have lost no ground, have saved time and money necessary to provide for the outfit, as well as having learned the avoidance of contingencies that might otherwise have rendered the experiment uncertain and disastrous. When I get ready, I am certain of success, but until then I have determined to publish nothing about the merits or difficulties of the enterprise.

There is plenty of room in the atmosphere for experimentalists in this unexplored art. I wish them all success and expect much information and improvements to spring from their trials, but I object to being ruled out of the field of aeronautic progress without my knowledge or consent. My own scheme is one of plain sailing—nothing but the balloon and water car. These, properly constructed, will serve the purpose of transatlantic, transpacific, and circummundane voyages.

John Wise

All that is known of the region into which the daring navigators of the *City of New York* are about to travel is that there is an air current, blowing steadily at a certain elevation from west to east. The travelers will of course make it their business to avail themselves of it. Should they gain it on starting, and keep it throughout their voyage, they would find themselves in Spain in the course of three days. Should the current deflect, or should they be driven out of their course by accident, they might land either in Great Britain or France on the north, or in Spain, Portugal, or Africa on the south. They propose to provide themselves with passports for all the leading nations of Europe, so that they may experience no difficulty. The flags on the balloon evidence the cosmopolitan feelings of the aeronauts.

The crew will consist of eight persons, as follows: the aeronaut, four scientific navigators, two scientific landsmen, and the historian. No passengers will be taken at any price, although the applicants are already numerous—several gentlemen offering large sums for the privilege of passage. Among the articles to be carried on the experimental trip are one hundred small parachutes, for sending down letters and papers to towns or to passing vessels; one hundred rubber mailbags for keeping letters and packages dry; one aneroid barometer; two marine compasses; a number of ordinary compasses, thermometers, and telescopes.

Besides this, a number of carrier doves will be taken out, and loosed from time to time, with accounts of the expedition around their necks. A disconnecting apparatus for the purpose of instantly detaching the boat from the balloon is provided, in view of an emergency requiring such a course of action.

Possibly Lowe may be obliged to take a sail in the ocean before reaching the shores of the Old World, and to make this part of the trip as safe and comfortable as possible, he has provided himself with numerous life preservers, and a Francis metallic lifeboat, capable of sustaining forty men in the sea, however rough. While the balloon is driving along at the rate of 100 miles an hour it is easy to see that considerable difficulty would attend a debarkation. Apparatus has been devised which Mr. L. says will so retard the balloon that it cannot progress at the rate of more than three or four miles an hour. Should necessity require the abandonment of the airship, it could be accomplished easily while going at this speed.

The entire weight of the balloon and the appurtenances is three and a half tons; its lifting capacity will be about twenty-two and a half tons. The following are the dimensions:

Greatest diameter, 130 feet
Height, from valve to boat, 200 feet
Capacity of gas envelope, 725,000 cubic feet

As it is expected to ascend to a height where cold is severe and perpetual, due precautions have been taken to protect the passengers from discomfort. A stove has been provided in which heat is generated by the slaking of lime. This apparatus will serve to keep the party warm, heat coffee, and perform such operations of minor cookery as may seem desirable. Of course no fire will be used about the machine.

A novel contrivance will be used to test the various currents of air. This will be nothing more than a cord, a mile and a half in length, kept out from the time the balloon starts. A careful inspection of the flags on the cord with a glass will enable the aeronauts to ascertain the direction of the various air currents beneath them. In case they happen to be in an unfavorable current, they can, with the guidance of the barometer, descend to a more suitable air stratum.

Staten Island, Monday, July 11

TO THE EDITOR OF THE N.Y. *Times: Sir:* I quite agree with your remarks with reference to the dangers of throwing out sandbags of ballast on aerial excursions. I think the remedy is very simple.

Let the requisite amount of ballast (sand, probably, being the most convenient and proper) be contained in a tank or compartment in the boat, with an adjustable valve attached sufficiently large to admit a rapid discharge when necessary. The discharge of weight could be much more delicately regulated than by throwing over bags containing a specific quantity of sand.

The boat might be built with double sides like a lifeboat, and the interstice used for ballast. The boat under this construction would also be more safe if unfortunately plunged into the water.

This arrangement would quite meet all the objections that you mention. I am, Sir,

Your most obedient servant,
John Smith

WATERTOWN, N.Y. Mr. La Mountain made a successful ascension in his balloon *Atlantic* at five minutes past four o'clock this evening. The air was still and he rose gracefully. . . .

Crossing the Atlantic in the air within two days is something of an enterprise; but why can it not be accomplished? Nothing seems impossible to the scientific genius of this generation which has accomplished almost miracles by the aid of science and art, from the simple, yet now indispensable lucifer match up to the wonderful daguerreotype and photographic process, which can represent in a second of time both a bombshell as it bursts in the air and one's own face on his coffee cup—an age which has laid the Atlantic cable, applied balloons to military purposes, and produced weapons of destruction that cut whole squadrons from a distance. Can anything be deemed impossible to the race which has achieved all these feats?

Mr. La Mountain landed his balloon at Hortle White Creek, Washington County, at 5:30 P.M. . . .

When the Atlantic cable was laid, the enthusiasm of this country went off at half cock, but when our aeronauts have succeeded in crossing the ocean in an airship, what excitement there will be at both sides of the world! The man who succeeds in doing it will be a wonder for a week.

Professor John La Mountain made his second ascension from Watertown today in his celebrated balloon, *Atlantic*. He was accompanied by John A. Haddock of the Watertown, New York, *Reformer*. Professor La Mountain's course was northward. . . .

* * *

Mr. La Mountain intends soon to cross the ocean in two days. However, he will make one or two more experimental ascensions, first from Jones' Woods, on the fourth of October, and the second from Albany on the eighth. We may send a special reporter aloft with him to furnish us with a correct description of the ascension, the speed of travel, the action of the thermometer and barometer, and all the phenomenon which may present themselves to his astonished gaze during the two-day trip, and perhaps furnish us with an intelligent criticism on "The Music of the Spheres." Accounts of this kind have often been given by aeronauts themselves, but we are going to find out now what a reporter's account of it will be.

Professor Lowe really seems to be more distinguished by a rash and daring recklessness than anything else. He has been encouraged, it seems, with funds or promises of funds, and has built himself a balloon almost as high and large as the Tower of Babel.

To look at his portrait, everyone must see the evidences of a pretty strong resolution and good courage. Beyond that, everything appears venturesome to the most terrible extent. He proposes, for instance, to let fall a string a mile and a half long armed with flags, by which to discover the various currents of air beneath him. But as he proposes to travel at not less than sixty miles an hour, it may reasonably be questioned if his flags and cord will not retard his progress—without the slightest prospects of doing good— if the current should be flowing different below from above. If this is a specimen of his wisdom and forethought, we cannot but fear he will be disappointed.

All the rest is planned on a large scale, but with no other advantages in improvement. We wish him success, and perhaps someday, someone will succeed in reaching the other side of the Atlantic. Lowe does as well to mouth the forlorn hope as anyone, but many will have to fall, probably, before one succeeds.

Providence, Thursday, July 14

TO THE EDITOR OF THE NEW YORK *Times:* The suggestions of your correspondent "John Smith," in yesterday's issue in reference to the best method of discharging sand from a balloon, are valuable and important, providing nothing else can be substituted. It seems to me, however, that we should look about for something far more appropriate; something that would answer every purpose as ballast and do no possible harm in its descent to *terra firma.* And I think water would answer every purpose.

The only objection that I can see to this plan is the difficulty of taking up sufficient quantity. But I apprehend that even this could be overcome by making what is called the car—which is generally, I believe, nothing but a large basket—of block tin, divided into compartments on the same principle that the hulls of many iron ships are now constructed. By this means, any quantity of water could be taken up, the car would be comparatively light, and if the aeronaut should be so unfortunate as to drop into a lake, he would perhaps find both safety and salvation in its buoyancy. Ample means could be devised for letting off the water, either slowly or rapidly, by means of common taps, and "mortals below," when looking up to witness the flight of the aerial ship would be in no danger of having their eyes filled with sand.

W.Q.M.

WATERTOWN, NEW YORK. MONDAY, SEPTEMBER 26: Nothing is yet known of Professor La Mountain or Mr. Haddock who made a balloon ascension here on the 22nd. Much alarm is felt for their safety. Their course when last seen was N.N.E.

WATERTOWN, NEW YORK. TUESDAY, SEPTEMBER 27: No tidings of the fate of Mr. La Mountain and Mr. Haddock, now absent after five days. When they were last seen, they had traveled only about thirty miles, and were at an altitude of about three miles bearing nearly east and over the New York wilderness. Search is being made there.

To the Editor of the New York Tribune —

Sir:

I have the satisfaction to say that I have received a telegram announcing the safety of Professor La Mountain. He is now at Kingston, Canada West, and will ascend from there tomorrow. The sale of seats for Thursday announced in your paper for the last week, will not be postponed.

Respectfully,

O. A. Ingersoll,
Agent

Mr. La Mountain will, therefore, be on hand for his grand experimental trip from Jones' Woods on the fourth of October, in the great balloon *Atlantic,* accompanied by a reporter for the *Herald* and other gentlemen who will purchase the choice of seats by auction of Mr. Nicholay, at the Merchant's Exchange, tomorrow evening.

* * *

There is little doubt that La Mountain and his companion are lost. It is now seven days since their ascension from Watertown in this state. The report printed yesterday that he had safely reached Kingston, Canada West, was entirely false, and originated in some inexplicable manner, for which Mr. Ingersoll, the New York agent, is not responsible. Yesterday, he telegraphed Mr. A. J. Morrison of the Troy *Daily Times,* who is Mr. La Mountain's agent in the city, and wanted to know if anything had been heard from the aeronaut, and received the subjoined dispatch: "Yes, he landed safe. Going up tomorrow from Kingston. He will be in New York by Friday."

Yesterday, however, Mr. Ingersoll received another dispatch as follows: "La Mountain not heard from. Mr. Morrison will write you today."

J. M. Travers,
Troy *Daily Times*

❖❖❖❖❖❖❖❖❖❖❖❖❖❖❖❖❖❖❖❖❖❖❖❖❖❖❖❖❖❖❖❖❖❖❖❖❖❖❖

New York, September 29:

In consequence of no intelligence having been received concerning the safety of Professor La Mountain, the sale of choice of seats in the balloon *Atlantic* is unavoidably postponed until further notice.

Albert H. Nicholay, Auctioneer

❖❖❖❖❖❖❖❖❖❖❖❖❖❖❖❖❖❖❖❖❖❖❖❖❖❖❖❖❖❖❖❖❖❖❖❖❖❖❖

Tuesday afternoon, says the Troy *Times,* a party embracing Mr. Edward La Mountain, brother of the aeronaut, several relatives of Mr. Haddock, and others, left Watertown to follow the route of the balloon as far as it was seen, and if possible to terminate the dreadful uncertainty that exists.

* * *

A reward is offered by his brother of $1,000 for the recovery of the aeronauts alive, $500 for their bodies if dead.

WATERTOWN, NEW YORK. SEPTEMBER 29: Professor La Mountain has been traced a little further. He was last seen in the town of Pitcan, St. Lawrence County, 50 miles due northeast from here, at a supposed altitude of five miles, going due east with great velocity.

ROME, N.Y. A rumor was current in our village yesterday afternoon, brought by the Watertown train, to the effect that a letter had been picked up in Canada "near a town, we believe," written by La Mountain, stating that Haddock was insane and that the rope was so tangled up that the valve could not be opened to let out the gas so as to allow the balloon to come down.

We give the story as reported at the depot. We will add that we placed no reliance upon it. . . .

* * *

The mystery grows more intense and painful from day to day. Here, in Troy, where he has relatives and many personal friends and acquaintances, the telegraph wires are watched with great anxiety, and as report after report is received announcing no further tidings of him, hope almost gives way to despair.

Mrs. La Mountain is stopping at a friend's in this city. We learn she is yet hopeful, and expresses far more confidence in her husband's safety than others claim to have.

Every genius finds that his success creates for him rivals and imitators on all hands. The particular novelty of the hour is decidedly that of aerial navigation, and the gush of professors of that science who have all at once sprung into existence is really startling.

This imitativeness is a very curious peculiarity in our national character.

Some months ago, Blondin's performance brought out quite a crop of geniuses whose talents in the highly meritorious accomplishment of tightrope locomotion had never been heard of before, even in their native villages. A few years ago there was as decided a rage for imitating the common housefly, and walking in an inverted position from ceilings. Sam Patch's renown also brought out a large supply of professors which, however, became considerably thinned off from accident in course of time. The ghastly body of the last of Sam Patch's imitators is still circling in the eddies of the whirlpool of Niagara. A frightful sacrifice of life resulted a few days ago in the village of Albion from the breaking of a canal bridge on which a crowd had assembled to witness a silly and ridiculous performance of the Blondin style. The rapids of the Niagara have been crossed on stilts; the feat of walking on the water has been performed on the Ontario; in fact it would seem as though the inventive genius of our people has been turned from all useful pursuits and applied with the utmost art to things that are in themselves absurd and ridiculous.

And in nothing has this curious tendency been made more manifest of late than in the matter of aerial navigation. The records of ballooning show the tragical fate of many an intrepid aeronaut whose life was the forfeit of his daring; but they fail to show that any important advance has been made in the way of making the navigation of the air a feasible thing. To be sure, a theory has been recently started in this country in regard to the existence of regular atmospheric currents, always moving in the same direction, at different degrees of elevation; and it has been suggested that, taking advantage of these currents, long voyages may be made with balloons from one country to another. That, however, remains to be proved.

It was to test this theory that the balloon *Atlantic* was built in which Mr. Wise and Mr. La Mountain made their famous trip last summer; and in which the last named gentleman ascended from Watertown last week, on that voyage among the clouds which, it is much to be feared, has added his name to the list of aeronauts whose fate has been tragical. That St. Louis trip created the greatest excitement, and has brought forth an immense crop of balloonists. Mr. Lowe is building a monster aerial ship over in Hoboken; Mr. Wise is giving a series of ascensions in Hamilton Park, with a view of creating an interest in the matter and getting the capitalists to engage in an enterprise similar to Mr. Lowe's. La Mountain has resolved to lead the way across the ocean, and as there was none more daring than he, the experiment would certainly have been made if he had returned safely from his last trip.

In the meantime, balloon ascensions have grown to be of a daily occurrence, and many who have had no experience whatever are rushing madly into the business. As a necessary consequence, we must expect to read of many deplorable casualties. In yesterday's *Herald* we had accounts of two ascensions which were attended with great risks to the aeronauts. In the one case, the balloon exploded; but in descending to the earth, it acted as a parachute, breaking the force of the fall. . . .

The aerial excursionists were perfectly cool, and conversed together during the descent. But for the few seconds after the explosion, when the car and the remnants of the balloon were swaying alternately above each other, their fears could not be suppressed.

In the other, the balloon was torn by coming in contact with trees, and those in the car narrowly escaped with their lives. The business is now in danger of being entirely overdone, and thus confidence in the final success of aerial navigation, instead of being increased, is being much diminished.

TO THE EDITOR OF THE NEW YORK *Tribune: Sir:* From all the circumstances of the case, I do not believe they are killed or totally lost. . . .

John Wise

State of New Jersey, July 18

TO THE EDITOR OF THE N.Y. *Times:* It is interesting to witness the inventive efforts put forth in regard to the "Ballast for Balloons," to save some luckless wight a cracked skull by a sandbag from one of the aerial ships. To contrive *"block-tin* cars with compartments for water, and taps to let it out," is about as sensible as the Atlantic Telegraph Company's contrivance of a brake to break the cable in the act of laying it.

Ballooning has not been improved since Montgolfier's time, and it is ballooning still—ascending in the air at the mercy of the winds, and descending again; a way of making money by exhibitions—nothing else.

Nobody has tried to navigate the air since the days of M. Charles. The attempts then were feeble, unmechanical, and unscientific. *No rational experiment has ever yet been tried.*

La Mountain, Wise, and Gager are balloonists. A tub will float up the Gulf Stream from the Gulf to Newfoundland, but can the ocean be navigated in a tub? The aerial navigation of those balloonists is all gammon—a misnomer to call any of them navigators. Ballooning is one thing; navigating the air another. Let us have the latter as something useful and worthy of effort.

Amateur

A dispatch was received in Troy Monday night dated, Ottawa, Canada West, Oct. 3rd as follows:

Lost all. Landed three hundred miles North of Watertown in the Canada wilderness. We were four days without food. Brought out by the Indian guides in canoes, etc. Please inform my wife.

John La Mountain

CHAPTER 10

But was it a practice flight? . . . La Mountain and Haddock tell their incredible and heroic tale — descent into the wilderness — two frogs, four clams, and a handful of berries keep them from starvation — help and rescue at last.

LANDING IN THE WILDERNESS

THE BALLOON ABANDONED

Four Days Without Food

LOST IN THE WOODS
ONLY RAW FROGS AND BERRIES

PROVIDENTIAL DELIVERANCE

Three Hundred Miles in Four Hours

La Mountain

I did not intend to go to Europe. I had no idea when I started of making a long voyage. I think I shall have no difficulty in explaining why it was that my designs were not carried out precisely as I had anticipated. The unkind remark of a veteran aeronaut—made at a time when he supposed me a dead man—that "fools rush in where angels fear to tread," is still not justified.

I had designed going up on Tuesday but the weather was so inauspicious that a postponement became unavoidable. Wednesday was no more propitious. Thursday opened stormily and unpromising, and I was in great doubt whether it was advisable to undertake the enterprise. But having another engagement on hand at Kingston soon, and being unwilling to disappoint the people who had so kindly awaited a favorable occasion, at about 12:00 I commenced filling. At 5 o'clock the inflation was completed, and as I saw the globe rounded to its equator with the pure hydrogen, I felt more confident than ever before of making a voyage with which everyone should be delighted.

At half past 5 o'clock, Mr. John A. Haddock, Editor of the Watertown Reformer, *who was to be my companion, took his place in the car with me.*

Many were the friendly hands La Mountain shook—many a fervent "God Bless You" and "Happy Voyage" were uttered—and many handkerchiefs waved their goodbyes.

170

Just as I stepped in, my good friend, Fayel, stripped off his overcoat and pressed it upon me, saying that, as Mr. La Mountain had no outer garment, we would need more than we had. I took it. It did me good service but I was never able to return it.

"Let all go!" and away we soared. The horses on the square reared and pitched a good deal at the novel sight, but in an instant, all minor sounds of earth had ceased and we were lifted into a silent sphere, whose shores were without echo. Not the least feeling of trepidation was experienced. An extraordinary elation took possession of my soul, and fear was as far removed as though I had been sitting in my own room at home.

As we rose, the light fleecy clouds between us and the earth looked like patches of snow lying upon the landscape in springtime; but when we rose higher, they completely shut out the earth. The cold white masses below us had precisely the same look that a snow-covered mountain country does as you look down upon it from a higher mountain.

Those who have crossed the alps by the Simplon Pass, or have stood on one of the lofty summits of the Sierra Nevada, and gazed upon the eternal snows below and around them, will be able to catch the idea I am trying to convey. In six minutes we were far above all the clouds, and the sun and we were face to face. The balloon rotated a good deal, showing that she was ascending with great rapidity. It struck the northeastern current and was drifting along at about the rate of twenty-five miles per hour. This current was one of great depth; although we went up to the height of three and a half miles, we did not lose it. After reaching that altitude, we took a still more easterly course.

At 5:48, the thermometer stood at 42, and was falling very fast. At 5:50, we were at least two miles high, and the thermometer showed 34. At 5:54, the thermometer stood at 28 degrees and was falling.

At two minutes past six, the thermometer indicated 31 degrees, having fallen 18 degrees after our departure from earth.

Mr. La Mountain directed me to throw about twenty pounds of ballast. This shot us up again. Thermometer was 26 degrees and falling very slowly. At 6:16, the thermometer was 22. My feet were very cold.

La Mountain   *Here, my friend Haddock, who had sat unconcerned in the basket, taking notes as coolly as though in his comfortable sanctum in Watertown, began to discover that it was rather too cold to propel a pencil. He, therefore, provided himself with the overcoat his friend had furnished him, and fortunately found in the pockets an extra pair of gloves for me—mine having been dropped from my pocket on the Square.*

The Atlantic *was now full and presented a most splendid sight. I here ate my first meal in three days—having been unwell during that time—and the last it was to be my good fortune to enjoy during the four days to come. Unfortunately for Mr. Haddock, the balloon commenced "blowing off" soon after; and this, with the attendant rarefication of air which had caused it, decidedly discomposed his stomach. The result was that we were somewhat lightened: he lost about all he had eaten. We were, therefore, neither of us in the very best of condition for the somewhat peculiar experiences soon to befall us.*

At this point, a suggestion made by Judge Clark just before starting was found to be a very good one. He had advised taking along some cotton with which to fill the ears when at great height, and my father had procured some. The unpleasant ringing sensation had now become painful. I filled both ears with cotton, and this made my head feel a good deal like a very large hollow pumpkin might be supposed to with a hummingbird buzzing about its face.

Haddock   Mr. La Mountain was suffering a good deal with cold. I passed my thick shawl around his shoulders and put the blanket over his knees and feet. We drifted along till the sun left us, and a short time thereafter the balloon began to descend. At 6:38, we threw over a bag of sand, making eighty pounds of ballast discharged. We distinctly heard a dog bark. The thermometer was at 28 degrees and rising rapidly. At 6:45, the thermometer was 33 degrees. At 6:50, it was dark and I could make no more memoranda. I put down my notebook, my pencil, and settled down into the basket, as much at home as though at my post in the Reformer office. From this point until the morning, I can only give my experiences from memory.

La Mountain   We remained upon the surface of the clouds, floating on them as a ship does on water. Mr. Haddock was very anxious to keep up, but I had already stayed longer than I had anticipated, and the number of my engagements had impressed me with the importance of making a safe landing before dark.

I opened the valve. The sun had just left us and it was hardly twilight up there. But as we went down, it became densely, impenetrably dark. The illusion was therefore borne out of a foundered ship, cleaving the waters on the way to the bottom of the ocean. To be sure, there was no difficulty in breathing. The atmosphere was quite warm; the only sensation one of oppression caused by the awful darkness. . . .

Haddock   Every light was extinguished, and every sound hushed into silence. The moon, to which we might have looked up for companionship and assistance, had she been present, was nowhere to be seen. The sky, at all times darker when viewed from an elevation than it appears to those inhabiting the earth, seemed *almost black with the intensity of night; while, by contrast, no doubt, and the remotion of intervening vapors, the stars, redoubled in their luster, shone like sparks of the whitest silver scattered upon the jetty dome around us. Occasionally faint flashes of lightning, proceeding chiefly from the northern hemisphere, would for an instant illuminate the horizon, and after disclosing a transient prospect of the adjacent country, suddenly subside, leaving us involved in more than our original obscurity. As we looked forward, we could scarcely avoid the impression that we were cleaving our way through an interminable mass of black marble in which we were imbedded, and which, solid a few inches before us, seemed to soften as we approached. Even the lights which at times we lowered from the car, instead of dispelling, only tended to augment the intensity of the surrounding darkness, and as they descended deeper, appeared absolutely to melt their way onward by means of the heat which they generated in their course. . . .*

La Mountain   *As we passed through the clouds, we heard a roaring of a great cataract. My impression was that it was one of the falls of the Ottawa, a short distance above Bytown.*

After we got clear of the clouds, we found to our astonishment that we were not more than five hundred feet above the earth and it was exceedingly dark. Directly under us, and as far as the eye could reach, was one unbroken, unpeopled wild. We were able to tell that we were over woods and not water, because we settled down so near the tops of trees that when I threw out a small quantity of sand, we could hear it rattling among the leaves and dry branches. It was a perfect calm at this time—about half past seven o'clock. Hardly a breath of air was stirring and the balloon did not sway in any direction. I could have made a landing with perfect ease, but there are always many objections to coming down amid timber, and I had no disposition to run the risk of damaging my splendid balloon.

Haddock

We heard a locomotive whistle, and occasionally wagons rumbled along the ground or over a bridge. The dogs kept up an almost ceaseless serenade, as if conscious that there was something in the sky, monstrous and unusual. Mr. La Mountain now said it was folly and madness to stay up any longer, that we were over a great wilderness, and the sooner we descended, the better. We concluded to settle down by the side of a tree, tie up, and wait until morning.

La Mountain

We made six attempts to land, at intervals of ten or fifteen minutes apart— the object being to ascertain whether we had as yet passed the woods. On the third descent, we came down upon the bosom of a little lake, shut in amid the almost impenetrable extent of trees. The car even touched the water, and we had our life preservers ready for emergencies, but the discharge of a very small quantity of ballast changed the course of the balloon and it quickly rose again. On the fourth attempt, we came down beside a very high tree and caught hold of its branches for a moment to look around. There was still woods as far as the eye could reach, and right before us a frowning mountain raised its beetling head, until it seemed lost in the clouds. So up we went again, journeying for a few moments very close to the treetops. On the sixth attempt, we came down near the top of a tall tree, of which Mr. Haddock caught hold.

Haddock

I grasped the extreme top which stopped our descent and we were soon fastened to it by the large drag rope.

La Mountain

I reached out my hand and felt of it. It was spruce! A very messenger of evil tidings. No spruce grew in the New York wilderness that I knew, and the hardy tree was native only of colder climates. We must, therefore, be in Canada. If this was so, we were in the great wilderness. This, I knew, was almost unbounded—its only known limit being the Arctic Circle. Therefore the sooner we stayed where we were, the better.

Haddock

Mr. La Mountain said, after he looked around, and made as much of an examination of the scenery as we could in the darkness and rain (it had rained the past hour), that the Atlantic was played out, we were far into the woods, and if we got out alive, we ought to be thankful.

We rolled ourselves in our blankets, and patiently waited until morning. The rain dripped down upon us in rivulets from the great balloon. . . .

Cold, wet, and rainy the morning broke, the typical precursor, we were to learn, of many mornings to be spent in these uninhabited wilds. We waited until six o'clock with hopes that the rain would cease; that the rays of the sun—by warming the gas in the balloon—would give us ascending power sufficient to get up again, for the purpose of obtaining a view of the country into which we had descended. The rain did not cease and we concluded to throw over all we had in the balloon except a coat apiece, the life preservers, the anchor, and the compass. Overboard they went—good shawls and blankets, Mr. Fayel's overcoat, bottles of ale and a flask of Cordial, ropes and traps of all kinds. The Atlantic, relieved of her wet load, rose majestically with us and we were able to behold the country below. It was an unbroken wilderness of lakes and spruce. We felt then that we had gone too far through a miscalculation of the velocity of the balloon. As the current was driving us still to the north, we dared not stay up, drifting further and further to that "frozen tide" from which we knew there was no escape.

Mr. La Mountain seized the valve cord and discharged gas and we descended in safety by the side of a tall spruce. We made the Atlantic fast by her anchor, and for a moment talked over what we should do. We had not a mouthful to eat. We had no protection at night from the damp ground, were distant we knew not how far from habitation, were hungry to start with, and had no earthly hope of raising a fire.

La Mountain   *After jumping out, I knew it was necessary to abandon the balloon, as we should have all we could do to find our way out of that almost impenetrable wild without any encumbrances. There was no alternative—the work of the Atlantic was done. I have known what it is like to be shipwrecked at sea, and to behold a vessel I had learned to love as my home, engulfed in the foaming waters; but I had never experienced anything like the emotion that filled my heart as I exclaimed, "Goodbye, old Atlantic, we shall never meet again!" It seemed like parting from an old friend in perfect health, with the full knowledge that he would never be seen alive again. Tears blinded my sight, and it required, I suppose, the same effort to enable me to leave the cherished "companion"—for so I had learned to look at it—of so many perils and so many pleasures, as it does for a father to tear himself away from the coffin of a beloved child. Perhaps it was foolish and nonsensical; if it was, I can only say I could not help it.*

The departure must be made, so off we started to seek civilization, deliverance, safety, home, and friends. We soon found that we could only make snail-like and most laborious progress. The bottom was soft; the bushes closely grown together and loaded with deposits of the previous night's rainstorm; and dense masses of rubbish lay in the way in every direction, having fallen from the trees—never perhaps cut since God first planted the wilderness.

After laboring on about three quarters of a mile, we came upon a creek, the general course of which was to the northwest, but exceedingly tortuous. Here, we found a rude wooden trap used for catching martens, a little clearing with indications of a fire at some past time; and a half barrel with marks, "Mess Pork —P. M. Montreal." This apprised us that civilized man had been upon the spot before us and also removed any uncertainty as to being in Canada.

A brief debate decided us to follow up the stream on its north bank, being much easier to walk in the grass and water along the bank than to crowd our way through the tangled bushes, and over the underbrush. After following the creek about two miles, finding my weight uncomfortably increased by water saturation, I removed my woolen drawers and woolen socks, tore off about six inches from the bottom of my pants, and threw away my hat, which was a serious impediment in going through the bushes. Having on only light gaiters, I retained them as protection for my feet.

We journeyed in this direction about five miles, when—could we believe our eyes!—a lumber shanty. Joy! Deliverance was at hand!

We found a small round stick of timber lying in the creek which we both mounted, and, cutting some elders, poled across the creek, landing wet enough upon the other side. Eagerly we rushed forward expecting to meet a human welcome. Oh, misery! It was deserted, and plentiful indications existed that many storms had beaten upon it since residents had occupied it. Here, too, we found several roads leading into the woods; all of which we followed to their ends, supposing we might find some men cutting timber. Disappointed again. All the roads terminated in those impenetrable wilds, and there was nothing to indicate human presence.

On one of these roads, we found two tiny white frogs. They were the first "food" we had seen in twenty-four hours. I never tasted a sweeter morsel in my life. Not hindquarters alone; we were not dainty; forequarters, head, bones, and all.

We had no means of kindling a fire to dry our garments. I tried to strike fire in the Indian fashion by rubbing two sticks together and by drawing a small piece of rope rapidly across a peg, but both failed. After using all my strength, I only got up a heat of about 100 degrees, so we crawled into the straw—it was dry—pulling it over our heads and faces in the hope that our breath might aid in warming our chilled bodies. But our rest was much broken by dreadful cold and chills. I think the most revengeful, stony heart would have pitied our condition then.

We held a new council. It was evident, we reasoned, that the creek we were upon was used for "driving" logs in the spring season. If, then, we followed it, we would in time get out the same way the timber went out. The roof of the shanty was covered with halves of logs, scooped out in a manner familiar to all woodsmen. These were light and dry, and would form an excellent raft. Why not, then, take four of these, tie them to crosspieces by withes and such old things as we could find around the shanty, and pole the structure down to that civilization which a sawlog ought to be able to reach? Such was the course adopted.

Haddock   We dragged the logs down to the creek and La Mountain tied them together, as he was evidently more of a sailor than I. We got underway and as we pushed off a crow set up a dismal cawing. We poled downstream about ten miles, came abruptly upon an immense pine tree which had fallen across the stream, completely blocking the passage of the raft. No other alternative was left but to untie the pieces and attempt to push them through, under the log. This was at last done. We tied the raft together again and poled her downstream into a lake some two miles

long, and through which we, of course, supposed the stream
passed, having its outlet at the lower end. We followed down the
northern bank, keeping always in shallow spots, so that our poles
should touch the bottom, until we arrived at the lower end of the
lake, found no outlet and turned back upon the southern bank
in quest of it. On reaching the head of the lake again, we found
the current of the creek turned abruptly to the right, which was
the reason for our losing it.

We felt happy to have found it again, and plied our poles like
heroes. We passed, during the day, the spot where we had first
struck the creek, and where we made a slight landmark which
might afterwards aid us in finding the Atlantic, should we ever
wish to do so in order to get her out. At night we did not stop,
but kept the raft going down through the shades of a forest
whose solemn stillness seemed to hold the unrevealed mystery

of our darkening future. About ten o'clock, it began to rain again. We stopped the "vessel" and crawled in under some "tag" alders on the bank. Our extreme weariness enabled us to get perhaps half an hour's sleep. We were too weary, too chilly, too sad; and we took advantage of the pause soon after twelve o'clock

when the rain slackened to pole a short distance, when the flood gates were reopened and the storm beat upon us once more.

Rising again (for it was easier to pole at night in the rain down an unknown stream than to lie on the ground and freeze), we pressed on for a couple of hours, until about three o'clock, when pure exhaustion induced us to stop again. This time we found a spot where the clayey bank lacked a little of coming down to the water. Onto the mud we threw our little bundle of straw, and sat down with our feet drawn under us, so that our bodies presented as little surface as possible for the rain to beat upon.

The wind sighed through the branches of the trees, and the feeble rippling of the creek was in mournful harmony with the ebbing flow of our lives and spirits.

We could not stand such an uncomfortable position long, and as daylight broke upon us (it was the Sabbath), we were poling down the stream in a drizzling rain, chilled to the very marrow of our bones—pale and hollow-eyed; and with those terrible sensations of ringing in the head, dryness of the lips, and parching of the throat that precede starvation. We had not slept over an hour in the night.

* * *

At eight o'clock, we came into a place where the stream canyoned, rushing over a stony bed, down a steep descent between high rocks on either bank. To get our raft down this place we regarded as hopeless. We tied up and examined the shore. Here again, we found unmistakable evidence of lumbermen, as they had evidently camped at this point. The rapids were about a third of a mile long and in all the rapids of the Black River, there is nothing so wild and romantic as these.

We descended the bank and thought it best to try our luck on foot. After traveling about a mile, we found the bank so tangled and rugged, and ourselves so much exhausted, that locomotion was impossible. So we concluded to go back, and if we could get the raft down a piece at a time, we would go on with her; if not, we would build as good a place as possible to crawl into, and prepare for death.

We went back, and after examining the stream attentively, concluded to try to get the raft down. I freely confess this the most trying and laborious work of a life of labor. Pieces would not float over a rod at a time before they would stick on some stone which the low water left above the surface, and then you must pry it over in some way, and pass it along to the next obstruction. We were obliged to get into the stream often, up to the middle, and there I several times fell headlong; our compass now frantically pointed in any direction. The water had unglued the case, and it was ruined. After long hours of such labor, we got the raft down, and La Mountain tied it together.

Today, we found one clam, which I insisted La Mountain should eat as he was weaker than I, and had eaten little or nothing on the first day. By this time our clothes were nearly torn off. My pantaloons were slit up both legs and our night wrestlings in the canyon had torn the skin from ankles and hands. We slept but little. It really seemed as though during the night we passed through the horrors of a dozen deaths. At daylight, we got up by degrees—first on one knee and then on the other—so stiff and weak we could hardly stand.

*   *   *

About ten o'clock, we found a broad northern stream, which we thought was the outlet we were seeking, and we entered it with great joy. Shortly after entering the stream it widened out, and assumed the form of a lake. We poled up the westerly shore for about seven miles but found we were again deceived. On our way up, Mr. La Mountain sang these pretty lines:

> "Cheer up your hearts, my men:
> Let nothing fright you;
> Be of gallant mind—
> Let that delight you."

His voice was hardly above a whisper, but the song was a source of great comfort to me. His, indeed, was a "gallant mind," which the extraordinary hardships and dangers of our position had not daunted. But when we found that all the weary miles of our morning travel had been in vain, and had to be retraced, my resolution certainly failed me for a moment, and I sat down upon the end of the raft, and felt like shedding one tear of genuine regret. Yet, we felt that our duty as Christian men was to press on as long as we could stand and leave the issue with God.

La Mountain *About twelve o'clock, we entered a large lake. Never more cheerless a prospect opened on mortal vision. Perhaps weeks must pass before we could find the outlet. And then—what then? Never mind; we went striking to the right; close to the bank, and poling—poling—poling along numerous bays and indentations. Eye never looked upon more magnificent scenery. Embosomed in a great basin scooped out amid noble hills; surrounded by beautiful evergreen trees; dotted with little islands; and reflecting the deep blue of the sky—a painter could not have had more noble study. But where was our brother—man? the curling smoke of human habitation? the welcome face of sympathy; the beaming eye of intelligence? Alas! without these, what would have been the most matchless scene in Nature's broad domain was cold, dreary, and somber, to two worn, starving men—lost in the trackless wilderness.*

It had been four full days since we ate a meal. All we had eaten in the meantime was a frog apiece, four clams, and a few wild berries whose acid properties and bitter taste had probably done us more harm than good. Our strength was beginning to fail very fast, and our systems were evidently about to undergo an extraordinary change. I did not permit myself to think of food. I thought of poor Strain's suffering on the Isthmus of Darien, where he, too, was paddling a raft down an unknown stream—but never believing he could have stood half the amount of suffering he did. But he had means to make a fire; we had none.

Mr. Haddock began to look upon our fate as sealed. He was brave as man could be. The thought of death had no terror for him. But he mourned to think of the desolation of his wife and family. How little we knew what God had in store for us! I cheered my friend as well as I could.

Haddock

We turned the raft around and poled her back toward the place where we entered the last lake. We had gone about a mile when we heard the sound of a gun, quickly followed by a second report. No sound was ever so sweet to me as that. We hallooed as loud as we could a good many times, but could get no response. We kept our poles going, and had gone about half a mile when La Mountain's attention was drawn to what I thought was smoke curling up among the trees on the side of a hill.

In a few moments the blue smoke rolled gently yet unmistakably above the treetops. We could hardly believe our senses, and credited anything favorable to our condition with the utmost caution. Our bitter disappointments had taught us that lesson.

My own eyesight had begun to fail me to an extent that I could not depend upon it when a long, steady gaze was necessary. He said it was smoke and that he thought just below it on the bank was a bark canoe.

We paddled the raft with the ends of our poles directly across the lake and made for the canoe. It proved to be a large one, evidently an Indian's birch turned bottomside up on the bank.

La Mountain

Under it was a gun, two coats, and a sack containing a dead duck. Mr. Haddock started to hunt up the owner, and I seized and commenced stripping the duck, intending to eat it uncooked. But that was unnecessary.

Haddock

I hallooed—a noise was heard inside and a sober-looking Indian came to the door. He drew me into the cabin and there was the head of the party, a sober-looking Scotsman named Angus Cameron. I immediately told my story. Imagine my sur-

prise when they said we were 150 miles due north of Ottawa—
in the dense, uninhabited forest whose only limit was the Arctic
Circle. In a word, we were nearly 300 miles in a due north
course from Watertown.

La Mountain   In less than five minutes an Indian boy
appeared upon the bank. I addressed
him first in English and then in French.
He answered in the latter and asked me to follow him. I did
so, hardly being able to drag my body along. About twenty rods
from the shore, amid the woods, I entered the shanty from which
the smoke had curled. God be praised! There was my companion

conversing with a generous-looking Scotsman; around him a number of athletic timber cutters near a table laden with carrots, potatoes, pork, and so forth—all the heart could wish for. We ate as sparingly at first as our stomachs were able to bear, and were more ravenous as we became stronger.

186

* * *

Here, let me state that the stream we came down with our raft is called Falliman's Creek; the large lake we sailed around is called Baskatong Lake, and drains into the Poaketong River. Mr. Cameron assured us that these streams are so tortuous and in many places so rapid, that no set of men could get a raft down, no matter how well they knew the country, nor how much provisions they might have. He regarded our deliverance as purely providential and many times remarked we would certainly have perished but for seeing his smoke.

After finishing up his business in the vicinity where we found him, on Friday morning, Mr. Cameron started on his return.

We stopped, on our way up the creek, at the place where we had erected our signal by which to find the balloon. We struck back for the place and in about twenty minutes found her impaled on top of four small spruce trees, very much torn. La Mountain concluded to abandon her. He took the valves as mementos and I cut out the letters "TIC" which had formed part of her name and brought it home with me.

At Dessert, we were a good deal troubled to obtain Indians to take us out.

Starting at seven in the evening, we traveled nearly all night through the forest over one of the worst roads that ever was left unfinished and reached Brook's Farm in the early morning, a sort of frontier tavern, where we slept a couple of hours. After breakfast we pressed on by stage to Ottawa which we reached at five o'clock on Monday afternoon. Our first rush was to the telegraph office. . . .

La Mountain *Several general conclusions and remarks will terminate this narrative, already too long.* "*Why did you permit yourselves to go so far?*" *will naturally be asked, to which we can only reply that the wind was exceedingly light when we ascended; we were very soon among the clouds, and consequently unable to take cognizance of our course, or to judge how fast we were traveling. Perhaps it is well here to remark that when you are sailing in a balloon you are utterly unconscious of motion unless you can see the earth. Nor can you tell by compass, in which direction you are traveling, unless you are sufficient of an aeronaut or an astronomer to judge from the shifting angles formed by certain stars. In a word, if you cannot see the earth, you cannot tell how fast, nor in which direction, you move.*

This will, perhaps, explain why we unconsciously drifted off in latitudes so remote. When we rose above the thick masses of clouds before sundown, we undoubtedly struck a rapid current which carried us northeast. It is my opinion that after we had traveled in this current, we struck another current, from a variation of our altitude, which bore us off to the northwest. When we descended near the earth the first time, we ought to have come down, but we were unwilling to land at night in the deep wood, even though we knew we were not far from habitations; and we thought it best to pick out a better place. This was our error, and it came very near being a fatal one to us—it certainly was to the Atlantic. In trying to find our "better place" to land, we were unconsciously up longer than we supposed, traveling in a current which swept us off to the north at the rate of one hundred miles an hour. We soon reached the country not pleasant nor proper to land a balloon in.

The loss, to Mr. La Mountain, does not stop with the loss of his balloon. He had several profitable engagements to fill, which must, of course, all go over, entailing disappointment to the public and loss upon himself. In his present condition, in poor health, and not "overly rich," I cannot but hope some capitalist will furnish him with sufficient means to carry on. Of course, the present mishap has not changed his views relative to ballooning, nor has it mine. Mr. La Mountain is a brave man; he probably does not know what personal fear is. Such traits will always command the respect of those who know that the fine temper of steel is only imparted after exposure to severe tests, before whose intensity meaner metals perish or sink, blackened and worthless. . . .

The missing gentlemen arrived safely in Watertown on Tuesday evening. Their progress from Ottawa was marked with the most extraordinary demonstrations of rejoicing. At Ogdensburg, a public reception was got up, at which nothing would satisfy the people but a speech from our friend, Haddock, recounting the perils of the voyage and the hardships encountered in the unbroken wilderness of Canada. On their arrival at Potsdam, an immense crowd who had got wind of their coming greeted them at the depot. Here, too, Haddock made a speech. Mr. La Mountain was so much exhausted by the privations of his journey that he was unable to speak.

At Canton, Gouverneur, Antwerp, and Evans Mills, similar

demonstrations took place. At Antwerp, the joy of the people at the safe return of the voyageurs found voice in the thunder of cannon, and other demonstrations of rejoicing. Mr. Phelps, the superintendent of the Potsdam and Watertown Railroad, who was on the train, kindly gave permission to delay the cars five minutes at each station, in order to allow the people to satisfy their curiosity and express their congratulations at the fortunate recovery of the aeronauts.

It remained for Watertown to cap the climax of this series of ovations. Hundreds, thousands of people thronged around the station on the arrival of the train—bonfires shot up a broad glare, rockets sailed on fiery wings through the sky—cannon belched forth the immoderate joy of the people over the safe return of their favorites. In front of the Woodruff House our voyageurs were seized by friendly hands and fairly carried into the house. Hundreds rushed to grasp the aeronauts by the hand, and to express the joy over their return. We never witnessed such great enthusiasm in any crowd.

After spending a few minutes with his family in the parlor of the Woodruff House, another demand was made upon Mr. Haddock. Washington Hall was crowded almost to suffocation by friends who were eager to hear from his lips some account of the voyage.

When Messrs. La Mountain and Haddock appeared upon the stage,

JOHN A. HADDOCK

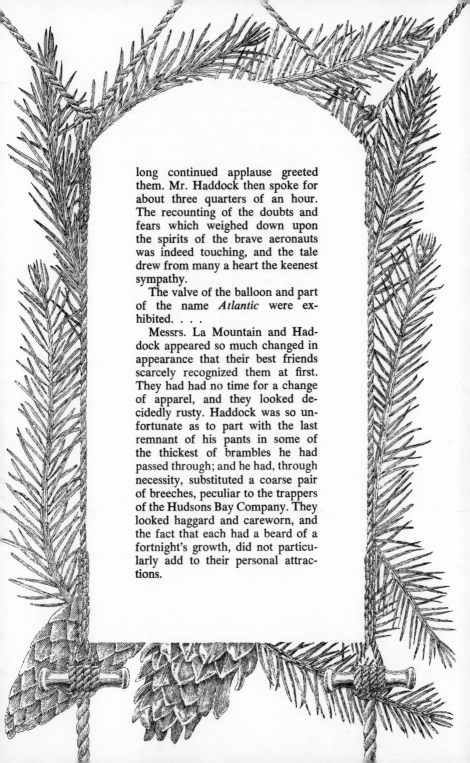

long continued applause greeted them. Mr. Haddock then spoke for about three quarters of an hour. The recounting of the doubts and fears which weighed down upon the spirits of the brave aeronauts was indeed touching, and the tale drew from many a heart the keenest sympathy.

The valve of the balloon and part of the name *Atlantic* were exhibited. . . .

Messrs. La Mountain and Haddock appeared so much changed in appearance that their best friends scarcely recognized them at first. They had had no time for a change of apparel, and they looked decidedly rusty. Haddock was so unfortunate as to part with the last remnant of his pants in some of the thickest of brambles he had passed through; and he had, through necessity, substituted a coarse pair of breeches, peculiar to the trappers of the Hudsons Bay Company. They looked haggard and careworn, and the fact that each had a beard of a fortnight's growth, did not particularly add to their personal attractions.

In personal conversation with Mr. La Mountain, he expressed to us his admiration for the bold and energetic conduct of Mr. Haddock. He declared that Haddock never faltered, but held bravely out to the last with a courage truly remarkable. He also expressed his profound gratitude to the people of Watertown and Jefferson County generally, for the many manifestations of friendship and kindness displayed in his behalf.

The entire damage by the loss of the balloon, both actual and prospective, is over three thousand dollars. Mr. La Mountain received about one hundred and fifty dollars from the receipts of the meeting at Washington Hall. . . .

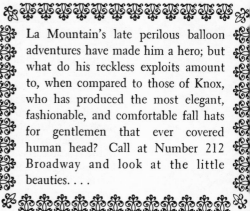

La Mountain's late perilous balloon adventures have made him a hero; but what do his reckless exploits amount to, when compared to those of Knox, who has produced the most elegant, fashionable, and comfortable fall hats for gentlemen that ever covered human head? Call at Number 212 Broadway and look at the little beauties. . . .

CHAPTER 11

The pros and cons of the La Mountain-Haddock flight in which feelings grow tense.

TO THE EDITOR OF THE NEW YORK *Herald: Dear Sir:* Permit me an opportunity to express my heartfelt thanks to the many generous friends who have extended to me their hearty congratulations on my escape from the Canadian wilderness. To those noble men who assisted Mr. Haddock and me to return in safety to our homes and families, I would say, God Bless you. And, finally, the Press, whose mighty influence was exercised to elicit an interest in our behalf and a thorough search for the "lost balloonists," has imposed upon me a debt of gratitude which I fear I can never repay. I have received many letters of congratulations, to which I am unable to make separate replies. Among others, the following from Mr. Hyde, one of the editors of the St. Louis *Republican,* which I should be glad to have you publish, not so much on account of its compliments for myself, as an answer to the sneers of one or two newspapers which have classed ballooning with ropewalking and other breakneck adventures. . . .

My Dear La Mountain—

Having participated in the general apprehension and concern relative to your late adventure, I assure you I am heartily glad to hear of your coming out alive, although sorry that your trip was so disastrous in other respects. You had had two narrow escapes, and as an aeronaut, your career has probably been the most eventful considering its comparative brevity. The life of a man like you, of undaunted courage and calculating intrepidity, possessing qualities besides which are more rare and not less manly, is too valuable to be lost in the depths of Ontario or away among the wilds of an almost interminable Canada forest. For the sake of your family and friends, for your own sake, and for the sake of the beautiful art of air sailing, I rejoice that the worst fears felt as to the termination of the voyage have not been realized. Do you know, La Mountain, that scarcely a day has passed since our cloud-cleaving, lake-shipping, and tree-thrashing ride of last summer that I have not, in some way or another, thought of you and Wise and Gager, and our wonderful rescue from the terrors of the storm? We all owe our lives to your presence of mind, coolness, and bravery; and I shall always feel deeply impressed with your conduct on that perilous occasion when you toiled and sweat to prevent our going down in those angry, lashing waves that seemed to leap up for the purpose of swallowing us all.

Whatever discouraging effect may have been produced by your recent unlucky adventure, I feel as convinced now that the dangers of navigating the air are overestimated by the public as I did when with unflinching step I got aboard the Atlantic in Washington Square, St. Louis, on the first of July last. Those who talk worst about the perils of ballooning regard the principal danger as being in midair, whereas you know—far better than I—it all lies in the landing; and under ordinary circumstances this can be regulated—effected with perfect ease and safety. Ships, which are commonly guided into port with system and precision, sometimes get the better of the navigators and pitch about at the mercy of the winds until they are wrecked and all aboard destroyed. Railroad trains occasionally run off the track, steamboat boilers explode, coaches upset, and horses throw their riders. Even pedestrianism has its perils, and in some sense, locomotion of any kind is unsafe. The first time I remember having experienced fear of railroad travel was when I got on the train at Adams, New York, and compared the jolting, jumping, clattering, banging, jostle of the cars with the smooth, noiseless, delightful (although almost imperceptible) motion of the proudly careering Atlantic. *Whether ballooning will ever come to anything of importance or not depends in a great measure upon the patience and assiduity of those who at present take the affirmative side of the question.*

You can afford to let people apply epithets to you and your projects, so long as you have the sympathy of your friends, which is more valuable than empty greatness. I have written this letter because I wish to express in some way my sincere pleasure in your safety. Trusting when you assay future voyages in the air (if, indeed, you have not been induced by your friends to forego the profession) that you may accomplish all you undertake and hoping your life may be long spared, I remain,

> *Very truly,*
> *Your friend,*
> *W. M. Hyde*

All air sailors appear to suffer the same things. Sometimes they are very cold, and then they put on their greatcoats. Sometimes they descend too rapidly, and then they throw their greatcoats overboard. Sometimes they are hungry and they eat. Sometimes they are thirsty and then they drink. Sometimes their noses bleed, and the nasal sanguification is recorded in the same sentence with the barometrical observations, if any happen to be made. Generally, they indulge in the finest writing about the appearance of the earth under them, of the stars above them, of thunderstorms in the distance. When they are in trouble they write, "Oh, Misery!" When they are out of trouble they exclaim, "Joy!" These are Mr. La Mountain's own expressions, but his "misery" seems to have been much greater than his "joy."

He appears to have been as joyous as, but much colder and a good deal hungrier than any other air traveler of modern times. That he was very uncomfortable, very much in want of his breakfast, in great need of dry pantaloons, and suffering generally inside and out, we verily believe. That he cried when he lost his balloon—as he says, "tears blinded my sight"—we can also believe; for the dear old *Atlantic* must have been a valuable piece of property. But is he not rather hyperbolical even for an aeronaut when he compares his emotions with those of a "father over the coffin of a beloved child"? "Perhaps it was foolish and nonsensical," he says. It certainly was, if he felt as he says he did. The cheerfulest part of Mr. La Mountain's narrative is when, safe and sound, he sits down to "a table laden with carrots, potatoes, pork, etc." He calls these honest eatables "a revulsion," and says that at first "it was altogether too much." However, he had the good fortune to "come to his stomach," which soon became "pleasingly ravenous."

Far more than a moiety of this aeronautic narrative is devoted to Mr. La Mountain's adventures, not in atmospheric limbo, but upon the solid earth. This, for the interest of science, is to be regretted. A gentleman with a passion for trouble and starvation, who wishes in the morning to be able to exclaim "Misery!" and in the evening to exclaim, "Joy!", can easily be gratified by missing his way for this purpose within a few miles of this city. When enthusiastic air voyageurs leave this honest old earth, we expect them to have the nosebleeds, to be cold, to be hungry; we expect them to be uncomfortable in the air, and hardly less so when they have landed. To read of these things at our "slippered ease" over the morning muffin and coffee is delightful to the sensitive mind. So is it delightful to read of a poor shipwrecked sailor tormented by Arabs or the wretched captured soldier scalped by Indians. But those of us who are the most eager for novelties do not ask any man brother to voluntarily submit himself to slavery or scalping for the sake of presenting to us a pleasing dish of horrors. Suppose that Mr. La Mountain should choose to enter a hot oven, calling the operation an experiment in natural philosophy! Are we to cry because he is taken out crispy and overdone? When Sir Humphrey Davy inhaled new and possibly noxious gases he ran a risk but not altogether foolishly; because if he had died, we should have known that the gas was deadly, and surviving the heroic experiment, he was able to give to the world an intelligible account of his sensations. But what has Mr. La Mountain to tell us? That he was cold? We knew he would be. That he was hungry? That, too, was probable. That he ascended with ease? Of course he did. That his descent was perilous? Who expected it to be otherwise? We defy anybody to find anything in his narrative of the slightest importance to science. He is no more valuable in his way than M. Blondin is in his. Both run great risks for the sake of money or notoriety.

It is easy to see that thus far the balloon is just where it was fifty years ago—a great, beautiful, fascinating toy. An aeronaut encounters now almost as many perils as the Montgolfiers did in 1783.

The voyage disproves what the St. Louis excursion was supposed to have proved, viz.: the existence of a permanent easterly current at a high altitude. They found no such current but on the contrary, were carried almost due north.

Evening Journal

TO THE EDITOR: This voyage did *not* disprove the theory of a permanent easterly current. So long as we remained above the strata of clouds, which hung over a mile deep, and within 500 feet of the earth, we traveled in a direction north of east. Every time we descended we were carried on the opposite angle. The *Journal* will understand that I think we journeyed first in the northeast current, probably 125 miles in a direct line from Watertown, and we should have gone an indefinite distance had we remained there. In *descending*, we struck a local current, which carried us beyond any question, southwest, drifting us back over our own track. Going still farther, on passing through the clouds, we were caught by the northern current and carried with it to the Canada woods. This stratum I do not conceive to have been more than 500 feet deep, and of immense velocity—unquestionably not less than 200 miles per hour. I have, sometimes in ascending to the easterly current, been carried first several miles in a direct northern line and then brought back southerly almost over the starting point. But I do contend that the "upper current" produced by the centrifugal motion of the earth in space blows invariably from west to east, and that it is affected by no meteorological phenomenon whatever.

As some journals have argued—judging from the point at which we landed—that the easterly current is not always reliable, I pause here to remark that I have never found it more reliable than on that Thursday afternoon. I thought then, and still continue to think, that had I maintained an altitude of two and a half miles, I could have crossed the ocean in thirty-six hours, and without any more ballast than an ordinary local ascension.

John La Mountain

TO THE EDITOR OF THE NEW YORK *Tribune:* When a man sees the same results 99 times out of 100 experimental investigations, he will logically infer that the results are the rule, and the exception the accident. Well, this ratio holds good both to the great eastward current as well as to the safety of ballooning. Out of 113 ascents in which I reached an altitude of three miles, the balloon sailed to the east 112 times. In the exception, she remained nearly stationary —landing three miles west of the point of ascension.

I have read Mr. Haddock's narrative with much interest and care. It seems to me strange that a person as well qualified in scientific observations as Mr. Haddock appears to be, did not use that intelligence in landing near where they heard a "locomotive whistle, and occasionally could hear wagons rumbling over a bridge, while the dogs kept up an almost ceaseless serenade."

Here, certainly, was a better place to come down, though it were in the woods, than to proceed into a more inhospitable country. Mr. Haddock must have been well enough acquainted with the nature of the region into which they were going. This was sheer recklessness—we cannot count it stupidity—and this must not be turned into an account of the "perils of ballooning."

Now, without wishing to detract one single iota of fame from this remarkable adventure, I must confess that it puts all of my ability and experience *hors de combat.* The ease and composure of this landing, by leisurely settling down by "the side of a tree, tie up, and wait until morning," when the balloon was rushing along at the rate of "over a mile per minute," is a feat in aeronautics that very much surpasses any claim that I could make. He says: "In a moment, we were near the earth, and as we fell, I grasped the extreme top of a tall tree, which stopped her descent."

Taking all of this now for sober truth, why should this remarkable trip disparage the uses of balloons? It only proves that the aeronauts were either reckless, or inconsiderate, or very ignorant of the geography of their country, and the hardships they endured should not be laid to the intrinsic perils of ballooning. Their northward track does not disprove the existence of the great western current. They sailed in the equinoctial gale and were for no length of time in the upper current. They made no barometrical notings, the only trustworthy way of telling height. The whole trip, as described by Mr. Haddock, goes to prove more for what I claim in the uses of ballooning than it does against it.

There is no new thing under the sun of the present day that is more abused than this noble art. The Press, in general, is down upon it with an unbelief in its utility. They have reason, I know, but that reason is too much based upon the absurd stories told by unfledged aeronauts and the inflated promises of the merest pretenders. There is not a more extended and magnificent field of exploration within the reach of man than that of aerial navigation.

I must close my letter, and will only ask for a little more time—time to enable the plans already matured to be put into operation; to evoke from the Press something more palatable than the present hopeless forebodings of an undeveloped art.

John Wise

TO THE EDITOR OF THE NEW YORK *Tribune: Sir:* I have read the lengthy letter from Mr. Wise, and feel that the veteran aeronaut whose reputation is as wide as the continent, and who has made hundreds of ascensions, should not have permitted himself to garble and pervert the positions assumed in my late statement to the public "for the mere apparent purpose of showing off his own superior wisdom." Permit me the privilege of setting the aeronaut right, and some general hints and suggestions on the subject of ballooning, even though emanating from an individual as humble and destitute of "scientific" knowledge as myself.

The day we ascended was cloudy—we saw the earth but once after we entered the bank of clouds, until we made our first attempt to land. There was little or no wind blowing on the surface of the earth when we left it, nor was there any wind blowing in any direction, when we performed the feat upon which Mr. Wise attempts to throw ridicule, of tying the balloon to a treetop. In the absence of all wind, what was to prevent our descending so gradually as to be able to grasp the top of a spruce and make the balloon fast? Whether or not this puts all of Mr. Wise's experience *hors de combat* is to me a matter of profound indifference; it is sufficient for me to know and state that such were the *facts.*

My account contains a careful notation of the fluctuation of the thermometer, more than can be said of any account ever presented to the public by Mr. Wise. Although he again indulges in doubts as to the truthfulness of my statement, the public will doubtless do me the justice to believe my notations of these fluctuations, since I could have no object in misstating them. It certainly was a great curiosity to me to witness the mercury steadily sink from 84 degrees to 18 degrees at the rate of about one and three quarters degrees per minute.

I expressly mentioned in my statement that our error was in not landing when we first came down to earth. Why, you may ask, did we not then land? Because we were *wholly deceived* as to the distance we had traveled; we supposed we had not then gone over 40 to 50 miles; we were unable to land the *Atlantic* in a forest, and as my statement further says, "we thought it best to pick out a better place, but this was our error."

Mr. Wise assumes that we were "rushing along at the rate of a mile a minute" when we tied up to a tree. When we traveled we were in upper currents—when we landed, we were wholly out of these currents and in a locality where scarcely a breath of air could be felt. Thus much for Mr. Wise's doubts and uncharitable sneers at my statement.

In speaking of his long experience, and the fact that all his ascensions have demonstrated the existence of an easterly current, Mr. Wise says: "These ought to be decisive arguments in favor of the safety of ballooning in *proper hands.*" Does he mean the remark as a fling at my friend, Mr. La Mountain, whose "proper hands," when the *Atlantic* was about to be dashed into the waters of Lake Ontario, rescued the party from death and earned a reputation which Mr. Wise himself said ought to be commemorated by a gold medal? I felt myself safe in such hands and should in a thousand voyages; for I do not believe a cooler head, more intrepid, nor more noble-hearted man ever sailed a balloon than John La Mountain; and I also believe that his knowledge of the great principles of ballooning is, today, superior to that of your distinguished correspondent. Of the St. Louis trip, Mr. Wise said he has "little to say." I should think not, under all the circumstances.

I think Mr. Wise once said, in a letter addressed to the public, that his business was to "make and sail balloons." Such, Mr. Editor, is not my calling. My business is to use printing presses. Would my brother printers consider me a good workman if I had a press which I could not work satisfactorily after twenty years' trial? And would they not think me a dull scholar if, after twenty years' experience, I could not point out some way in which profitable and desirable improvements could be made on the machinery? How was it with Mr. Wise and his ballooning? Can he point out improvements which he has made, or is the whole "science" just where Mr. Wise found it? Are not the vast, untraversed fields of space which surround the earth as far beyond the reach of aeronautic skill as when Montgolfier first flew his paper balloon in France?

When traveling in a balloon, you are utterly unconscious of motion unless you can see the earth; true, you may be able to see the North Star, or you may have a compass, but you cannot by these aids take cognizance of your course, unless you have a fixed object—the earth—to aid you in your observances. After twenty-four years' experience in building and flying balloons, our critical aeronaut, who does not believe in spruce trees nor in thermometrical speculation, has never invented any method by which travelers in a balloon may note their course and rate of speed on a cloudy day, or, for any cause, are out of sight of the earth. Yet this man is the champion aeronaut of America, and perhaps the world. What would be said of the men who made pretensions to "scientific" knowledge in any other department of learning, who manifested so profound an indifference to the first steps in the accomplishment of their theories? They would be pronounced charlatans, quacks.

Let me, in all kindness, suggest that our good friend, Mr. Wise, devote himself to the completion of some instrument which shall serve the purpose I have named, even though his labors shall deprive the public of some of his long-winded letters to the Press.

Can the air be navigated, and if so, can such navigation be rendered advantageous to man? That is a great question, and I shall leave this discussion to abler pens and more "scientific" heads than my own. To navigate the air without a gliding apparatus seems to require a steady current, upon which the aeronauts may implicitly depend. I do not believe that such a current exists, except perhaps near the equator. Mr. La Mountain thinks he traveled in the easterly current, and we may have done so—varying our course as we varied our altitude. But how, as ballooning is at present conducted (and as it always has been conducted), is the aeronaut to know with certainty *when* he is in that current?

I respect Mr. Wise, for I believe he possesses a certain amount of skill in ballooning. But he will excuse the American people—and I trust will recognize me as one of them—if they demand from him something more definite as regards his favorite theory than he has as yet advanced. With him, however, I agree that our late voyage disproves nothing. It merely demonstrates the fact that a man is lost, when in a balloon, the moment he loses sight of the earth.

John A. Haddock

TO THE EDITOR OF THE NEW YORK *Tribune: Sir:* Mr. Haddock thinks we are compelled to "go it blind" when we get above the clouds, because he and his friend got into a wilderness; and hence infers that ballooning is not advanced beyond what their experienced troubles would speak for it. Let me explain:

Before we ascend and when we are rising, we can see which way the clouds are moving, and when we become involved with the clouds, we know we are moving with them. Now, when we rise above them, and they appear quiescent beneath us, we are still moving in their direction and with their velocity. Should the current above move faster or slower, there will be a relative diverse motion apparent in them. Should we enter a current moving at an angle with the clouds, we again have the course and velocity of our airship pointed out. The experienced aeronaut, like the experienced seaman, will, by intuitive reasoning, tell the course and speed of his vessel by these observations. Experienced aeronauts become as familiar with clouds as do old marines with gulf streams, fogs, and seaweed.

My good friend Haddock will thus see that a quarter of a century of experience *has* taught me something in the art and something hopeful enough to write letters for the public's information. I have also invented the "collapsing cord," a device which enables the aeronaut to render his balloon powerless in an instant—a very necessary contrivance in bringing down a balloon in stormy weather. This would have been put into the *Atlantic* before we sailed from St. Louis, had there been sufficient time. I have used the collapsing cord to explode my balloon when 12,000 feet high, and within three miles of Philadelphia before thousands of spectators. Some of the newspapers predicted certain destruction if attempted. I did this to show that balloons would inevitably become parachutes in case of their rupture when aloft. I have authentic records of thirteen balloons which have bursted or collapsed while aloft and in no single instance were the aeronauts damaged in the least.

It is an interesting and delightful experiment to have the balloon suddenly collapsed when a mile or two high above the country. I know that many of your sober-minded readers will call this "enthusiastic," if not madness, but it is nevertheless true, and logical, as to its self-preservative action. I am almost afraid to tell what balloons can do, or what can be done with them as I am frequently assailed as a rash, daredevil-tempered man, for demonstrating truth that science points out in the art of ballooning.

The vast, untraversed fields of space which "surround the earth," are *now* within the reach of aeronautic skill, but the world is slow in adopting and using the means. It has ever been so. The pioneers of all important achievements get more censure than encouragement in their pursuits. Much of this, however, is caused by the counterfeits practiced upon the public which always have a tendency to depreciate the genuine investigation. I know I can make more money by taking up elephants, horses, and bulls, than I can in purely scientific explorations. But as that would militate against the dignity of science, I have thus far abstained. I am not sure that I will not resort to it in order to raise the necessary means for my circummundane outfit. If I do, the exhibitions shall be made classical, at least, and fit for the educated and elite of society to look at.

Mr. Haddock wants to know how we are to tell when we get into the easterly current. If my experiences in barometrical notings of fifteen years are worth anything, I can confidently say: always when your barometer falls to seventeen inches. Out of one hundred trials, this holds good. But any experienced air traveler can tell when he is going east without a barometer.

We are just learning about these things, and, once generally understood, they will serve us to sail through the ocean of the air above us with much more comfort and pleasure and far greater speed than we can on the oceans of water.

I shall never enter into a controversy upon the scientific merits of aerial navigation; yet, I am displeased as to its progress in the hands of those from whom the public have a right to expect something. My nature is never to say anything except what is a matter of fact, or that which is self-evident scientific truth.

John Wise

In our judgment, man was never designed to journey among the clouds, or he would have been provided with wings like the fowls of the air, instead of being left to his own imperfect resources and still more imperfect knowledge, to construct airships to be rent in two in the treetops, or driven to destruction by the elements.

It is a good way perhaps, to test one's courage and contempt of life, but that is all.

CHAPTER 12

Professor T. S. C. Lowe's great balloon, The City of New York, is made ready for its transatlantic flight . . . More of the raptures of balloon flight and the discouragements of a balloon on the ground . . . The transatlantic voyage by free balloon is never made, but these aeronauts have been a factor for the future.

EXHIBITION
EXTRAORDINARY
BALLOON · BALLOON

Inflation of the Grand Aerial Ship

CITY OF NEW YORK

THE LARGEST BALLOON EVER CONSTRUCTED

Now Open Every Day Till Further Notice

FROM 9 A.M. TILL 5 P.M.

PREVIOUS TO
ITS GREAT
AERIAL
VOYAGE
TO

EUROPE

AT THE CRYSTAL PALACE GROUNDS

THESE GROUNDS HAVING,

BY A VOTE OF THE COMMON COUNCIL,
BEEN GRANTED FOR THIS GIGANTIC,
SCIENTIFIC, AND WORTHY ENTERPRISE.

ADMISSION . . . . *25 CENTS*

Family Tickets, admitting six persons $1

N.B. — Due notice will be given of the day of ascension.

A month ago New Yorkers were astonished to learn that a balloon was in process of construction which, when inflated, would overtop Trinity steeple a hundred feet, and embrace within its capacious diameter a building nearly as large as that occupied by the *Times;* that this monster would need 725,000 cubic feet of gas to expand its canvas sides to their full dimensions; and more than all were they surprised to learn that the balloon was designed, not for trips across the continent or into the Canada wilds, but for sweeping over the ocean. Mr. La Mountain's recent disaster, and the thrilling story of his sufferings, have for a time caused this enterprise to be forgotten. It has been progressing, nevertheless, quietly and steadily. . . .

The aeronaut in charge is Mr. T. S. C. Lowe, a New Hampshire man, who has made thirty-six balloon ascensions. . . .

❧

We have received the following letter from Prof. Lowe. It will be observed that he reposes great confidence in the efficacy of the apparatus he has devised for the accomplishment of his undertaking, and avows his determination, in case of disaster, to repair damages and try again. His letter will be read with interest.

❧

29: In yielding to the request of friends who have desired me to make some explicit statement of my purpose in undertaking a transatlantic voyage, I deem the occasion appropriate for an expression of my views on the art of ballooning.

214

It is my intention to cross the Atlantic with a view to practical experiment and careful observation, and whether the attempt shall prove a success or a failure, it will at least have served the purpose of throwing new light upon the theory of aeronautics.

The impression seems to have become prevalent that no essential improvements in the art of ballooning have been effected since the era of the experiments instituted by the brothers Montgolfier, that the efforts of modern aeronauts have resulted in no decided advance upon the discoveries of the last century, and that no practical effect can follow the most successful attempts to navigate aerial vessels.

The skepticism fails to do justice to the parties who have given their time and attention to the science of aeronautics, for while it is admitted that the progress of the art has been slow and that the intricacies of a delicate problem have not yet been fully mastered, it would be idle to deny that our knowledge of the currents of the air has been greatly enlarged by practical experiment, or that an actual improvement has taken place in the construction and management of balloons. That no more rapid progress has been made is perhaps due to the fact that seven eighths of the persons engaged in the pursuit of the art are not practical investigators but merely exhibitors whose highest ambition is satisfied by pecuniary reward and whose essays in ballooning are confined to limited ascensions. During the past fifty years at least three thousand balloon ascensions have taken place in different parts of the United States and, including aeronauts, some eight thousand persons have made aerial voyages. While the experiments in ballooning have most commonly been conducted by inexperienced persons, but a single life has been lost and that catastrophe was occasioned by sheer carelessness. I refer to the case of Mr. Thurston.

I do not claim the credit of originating theories on the existence of air currents. Twenty years ago Mr. Charles Green, a veteran aeronaut, declared that a continual current from west to east always existed in the atmosphere; similar observations were subsequently made by French aeronauts; and Prof. Wise discovered the current in the course of his early experiments. My own experience has verified that theory. Later investigations, however, have proved that this easterly current does not always exist at the same altitude. It is by seeking this great air current that the transatlantic voyage must be accomplished.

No aeronaut will claim that balloons can be made useful for local travel so long as we are obliged to depend upon the process of displacing air for lifting the burden. But for long voyages and for crossing the Atlantic, nothing, I think, can be better than the common balloon provided with attachments like those I have already invented or something better for the same purpose.

No single individual developed the scientific apparatus of steam power, or brought the magnetic telegraph to its present state of completeness, and the same remark applies to the art of ballooning. It is time, however, that someone should make a bold push permitting the world to give its verdict as it will, and endeavor to effect some practical demonstration which shall revive the spirit of inquiry and investigation. If nothing is done but to talk and theorize or to make an occasional excursion, the aeronautic art will ever remain where it is.

Some people may think that I am insane, rash, or a seeker after fame, but this is not the case. I have for three years coolly considered the subject and have provided for every contingency. I intended to make my first trip across the ocean entirely a private undertaking, but, finding that the amount of expense to be incurred would overtax my personal means, I have been compelled to announce a public exhibition while preparing for the voyage.

It is true I would have preferred another season of the year for undertaking the first great experiment of transatlantic aerial navigation, but should the first attempt not prove entirely successful, I shall not be discouraged. If aerial navigation is ever perfected it will be accomplished by perseverance even in the midst of opposition and detraction. I am willing to take the risk and if I can do anything to add in however small a measure to the store of our scientific knowledge, I shall feel amply rewarded.

I cherish a fervent hope that the time is not far distant when we can travel in the air without the aid of balloons for a buoyant force. I have already devised a plan for an aerial carriage which can be navigated at a high rate of speed as soon as a propelling power can be discovered the weight of which shall be but one third of that we now employ. It only requires some shrewd and intelligent inventor to do this and aerial navigation will become a practical science.

T. S. C. Lowe

Bannister

The days in getting the machine ready —the nights he spent consulting the winds! Thrice he filled the balloon; three times he was seated in the basket, where I have seen him lying down, brokenhearted; and three times the inconstant winds rejected his vows and destroyed his hopes.

The populace, as it is everywhere, was an impatient, impetuous, and cruel tyrant. A disappointment is an offense, whatever be the occasion; and offenders, in every degree, are punished with the same species of injustice.

Thus, after our landing that day, his affections were afloat and in unison with the whole country, whose transport and admiration now seemed boundless. He bid them therefore to keep clear, and he would gratify them by ascending directly in their view. In vain I implored him against it . . .

Mr. Lowe and several assistants are actively making preparations for the inflation of his immense airship, the *City of New York* at Reservoir Square. Three 4-inch gas pipes connect three different street mains with a gigantic station meter, through which the gas passes into the balloon. The meter is seven and a half feet long, by eight feet in diameter, and weighs about four tons. This meter will register at the rate of 100,000 feet per hour, were it possible for the mains to deliver it in feet. In case this can be done, Mr. Lowe will soon be able to start for Europe.

When we first conceived the idea of making a balloon, he had never seen an ascension with one nor had I any practical knowledge of its construction. In the spring we resolved to build one on a very economical plan. Neither our fortunes nor our economies had ever allowed us to be in affluence; and we therefore entered on any business requiring expense with some disadvantage. . . .

Mr. Lowe was not able to commence the inflation of his monster balloon yesterday morning as was expected, on account of some unforeseen delays. The boat that is to be attached to the balloon has not yet arrived, and the large gas pipes that will conduct the required gas from the subterranean pipes in Forty-second street to the middle of the Crystal Palace Grounds are not yet fully laid. The process of inflation will not be commenced until next Monday, when the grounds will be opened to the public.

Business in the vicinity of Reservoir Square is preparing to look up. An attraction is preparing within the high fence which encloses what was once the site of the Crystal Palace, that will gather as large crowds as ever visited the spot in the golden days of the World's Fair; and wherever there are large crowds there also is business brisk. Proprietors of saloons thereabouts are decorating their places of business, hanging out larger signs, and laying in stores for a vigorous siege of hungry and thirsty sight-seers; directors of city railroad companies and proprietors of stage lines whose routes, at some points, are contiguous to the neighborhood, are rejoicing in the anticipation of increased gross receipts. All, in short, are laying plans for the event and congratulating themselves.

Outside of the fence, which is thirteen feet high, at every other chink yesterday, we found an urchin itching to get a sight of the mysteries within; and at each of the three entrances there were small congregations of the curious all day long, peering in at the doorways whenever an opportunity offered, regarding with inquisitive eye the burden of every cart that entered, and ready to ask innumerable questions of all who issued forth.

The work of preparing the ground has been in progress for three weeks. Now, however, all the rubbish has been removed. Beneath a tent in the center of the enclosure, concealed for the present from the public gaze, are the balloon and its appurtenances. During the time occupied in the inflation of the balloon and after the grounds are thrown open to the public, the caloric engine attached to the boat will be in motion every day.

The postponement on Wednesday was made because of the indication of a storm which Prof. Lowe had ascertained by barometrical observations was at hand. The snow which fell on Wednesday night accumulated so heavily on the tent that it was borne down by the weight. No damage, however, was done to the airship beneath it. Yesterday the matter of fastening the valve to the top of the balloon was completed. It is a beautiful piece of mechanism; the framework is of mahogany and the two lids are of cedar. It is three feet eight inches in diameter and weighs thirty-five pounds.

It was merely idle curiosity, as the world calls it, that took me into the air. I had seen a great metropolis under almost every aspect. I had dived into holes and corners hidden from the honest and well-to-do portion of the community. I had sought out the haunts of beggars and thieves, and passed hours communing with them. I had seen the world of the city below the surface as it were, and I had a craving to contemplate it from far above— to behold the immense mass of vice, avarice, and cunning, of noble aspirations and humble heroism, blended into one black spot; to take, as it were, an angel's view, and see the whole dwindle into a heap of rubbish on the green sward—to swing in the air far above all the petty jealousies, heartburnings, small ambitions, and vain parades, and feel for once tranquil as a babe in a cot; to find, as you drink in the pure, thin air, the blood dancing and tingling through your veins, your whole spirit becoming ethe- realized; to feel yourself really, as you had ideally in your dreams, floating through the endless realms of space, enjoying for a brief half hour at least a foretaste of that Elysian destiny which is the hope of all.

To see, to think, and to feel thus was surely worth some little risk, and this it was that led me to peril my bones in the car of a balloon.

The Great Balloon—this great machine, with all its accessories, is now on exhibition at Reservoir Square. Mr. Lowe, with his assistants, are busy making all the concluding preparations. The gas was not started yesterday on account of the portentous aspect of the sky. As soon as the weather promises fair, the inflation will be commenced. Meantime, the balloon, the lifeboat, the caloric engine, the wind fans and other appliances are open to the inspection of the public, on payment of 25 cents each.

On the occasion of our second voyage, after coming down, we offered to let some persons go up the length of a rope, which the bystanders, everyone of them refused to accept.-

At this time a rustic-looking country girl came along from town, where she had been at the ascension, and was invited by me to take a seat in the car, which she did, and was soon let up two or three hundred feet, much to the amusement of the bystanders. After hauling the machine down and handing the young lady out of the car, I prevailed on a trumpeter who was now standing by with his instrument to make a similar adventure. He did, and when up, gave a few blats on his instrument which acted like magic in bringing the people across the bridge from the town. Upon this a perfect mania ensued among them to get into the car and ascend the length of the rope, which was four hundred feet long, some going the whole length, others not aspiring to more than half and some even less, shouting their impressions to the gaping faces down below. . . .

220

The work of inflating the great transatlantic balloon began yesterday in Reservoir Square, in the presence of a number of spectators. The neck of the balloon was drawn toward the pipe and—the valve ropes of small cotton cord having been adjusted—was placed over the pipe and drawn tightly. The balloon was then folded in such a way as to gradually expand the case. On the folds, heavy bags of sand were placed to keep them down. This having been done, the network which is to be thrown all over the balloon, and to which the basket and the boat are to be attached, was so dispersed that there might be no entanglement as the inflation proceeds and the balloon acquires its ascensive power. The gas was turned on at half past 12 o'clock and instantly rushed through the ten-inch pipe in a dense volume. In a very few seconds the entire neck of the balloon was filled, and the body of the balloon began to swell . . .

Having first charged nothing, the business got too pressing, upon which a quarter of a dollar was levied; and this not abating the pressure of business, it was raised to half a dollar per ride, at which it was kept up until we had realized eighty dollars and were only then compelled to close the "fun" on account of the immense throng which had surrounded the balloon making further operations in this way impracticable. Some paid for two and even three trips before they left the car.

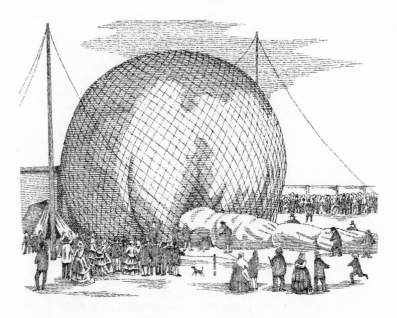

The precaution of stationing men all along the length of the balloon was by no means useless, as they had quite enough to do to remove the weights from places where the passage for the gas was too small, and so to adjust the folds of the cloth as to secure an equable passage throughout. At 12:35, the gas had reached the head of the balloon, which began to expand. If the process of inflation was continued at the present rate, without interruption, it would be fully inflated in six hours and a half. The only drawback, and a great one, is that the supply of gas by the company would not be equal to the task, as it would not do to leave the city in darkness for the purpose of inflating a balloon. Mr. Lowe will, therefore, be compelled to take his gas in such quantities as the company chooses to furnish. The process of inflation will be continued for some days.

Then the two of us clambered in. I began the ritual of finding equilibrium. Hands were raised. Hands were put back on the basket's rim. A sandbag was removed. Hands were lifted off again, and then replaced. Half a bag went overboard. . . .

222

After the gas had been flowing for some time, it was turned off, in order to afford Prof. Lowe an opportunity of adjusting the case, and to search for imperfections. None, however, was discovered although there was a very sensible smell of gas, which led some persons to believe that there was a leak. This supposition was strengthened by the fainting of a man who was assisting and became overpowered by the odor. He was placed under the small tent within the enclosure where the process of inflation was going on and the proper restoratives were applied.

At 11 o'clock, there being 32,700 cubic feet of gas in the balloon, the gas was again turned on, and the expansion proceeded.

At 11:40 the register indicated 36,500 feet. At this time the gas pipe was delivering one hundred cubic feet every forty-five seconds.

It will be perceived that there is a great discrepancy between this statement and that of Tuesday, which made the volume of gas passing into the balloon 7,500 feet in four minutes. This error arose from the stupidity of one of the men connected with the gas meter, in insisting that a cipher ought to be added to our reporter's correct note of 750 feet.

We shook hands with those close around, who were now grin-
ning hugely, and said farewell. Where they could find us and
when, and how, was another matter. That was for the winds to
decide. . . .

> The inflation of the great airship
> goes steadily on. Last night at six
> o'clock it was about one-tenth full.
> About 3,000 people visited the
> grounds yesterday to see it.

"Hands off!" I said to the men.
They did so and we stayed, toppling slightly on the ground.
"Hands on again, and take this sack."
They all clutched at the wicker rim, and one man dumped the
sack heavily at his feet.
"Hands off!" I shouted again, and this time we moved a few
yards before sliding along on the ground.
"Hands on!" and they all came running up. I gave one man
another sack.
"Hands off again!" I shouted, ridiculously loud, and at the
same time pulling a rope to let the balloon's mouth open, thereby
changing it from a sealed container into one where the gas could
expand. . . .

> Prof. Lowe states that on Sunday in consequence of the prevalence of high winds, it became necessary to discharge nearly the whole of the gas in the balloon, in order to secure it against the action of the wind. As his present object is, however, to test simply the capacity of the canvas, which will cause frequent discharges of the gas before a final inflation is made, no delay may be regarded as resulting from such an occurrence. At 1 o'clock yesterday morning the gas was again turned on, and up to 5 P.M., over 105,620 feet had been introduced.

Twelve men should find no difficulty in restraining the basket of a balloon, but on occasion in the past the helpers have panicked. If one man lets go, the remaining eleven wonder if it is still safe to hang on. So there may soon be ten, and that increases the chances of there being only nine. Before the captain knows what is happening, the others are letting go, and the final man is likely to be whisked into the air. Provided he lets go soon enough, only a balloon is lost. If he loses his nerve and hangs on, he is as good as dead. . . .

The process of inflating the monster balloon, the *City of New York,* is proceeding slowly but steadily. Thither thousands go daily to witness it, and to examine the lifeboat, the basket, the caloric engine, the lime stove, the anchors, the drag, the copper float, and other apparatus to be used in the aerial voyage to Europe. All these are on exhibition beneath the tent into which the visitor enters, immediately after passing into the enclosure. The boat, which is a staunch-looking craft, attracts much attention. Prof. Lowe himself watched its construction very closely and pronounces it an excellent piece of workmanship. On its sides are painted the words, "Leontine, New York." It bears this name in honor of Mrs. Lowe. Attached to it are the appliances for raising and lowering and changing the course of the balloon. The caloric engine is kept hard at work all day long. It is of four horse-power and weighs 35 pounds.

This morning a gentleman asked Prof. Lowe if he really intended to go to Europe. He replied that when the balloon is fairly up in the air, she cannot help going there.

The platform on which the boat and the engine are placed is draped with American flags, and on either side of it the other articles on exhibition are arranged very tastefully. A great many stop to examine the fur coat, cap, shoes, and gloves which Prof. Lowe is to wear in the cold regions of the upper air, and the robes and blankets which he is to carry with him. There is nothing remarkable in their appearance or construction, but they are interesting because they serve to remind one of the discomforts which the aeronauts must provide against.

The upper portion of the balloon is expanded to its full breadth and already rises several feet higher than the fence that surrounds Reservoir Square; so the outsiders who look through the openings in the boards can really see something within, and their number is largely increased . . .

Instantly, the miracle of a flight started once again. Without a bounce, without any apparent movement, we were flying into the air. We said nothing to harm those first few moments when the incredible repeats itself and a balloon takes leave of the earth with a grace that is unforgettable. Up, up we went, and smaller grew the people. How minute they were! How remote already! And how inaccessible!

Our point of no return had already been reached. As if by a signal we turned round in the basket and looked ahead to see what Chance and Fate had in store for us.

Prof. Lowe is personally superintending the work of inflation, and is constantly on the ground. He is, of course, the center of attraction. The visitors are as respectable in appearance as in numbers; they obey implicitly the injunction to stay without the rope barrier which divides the space set apart for the spectators from that appropriated to the balloon and its appurtenances. Several policemen are stationed on the premises to preserve order; their task has been a very easy one.

Among the visitors today were a number of ladies who seemed to take a great interest in the matter. They asked and demanded explanations in their peculiar polite way of the wicker basket, the caloric engine, of the Francis metallic lifeboat, and whether the aeronauts really intended to steer it through the air.

The precise day of Prof. Lowe's departure is not fixed, but he gives every assurance that he will go, and appears to entertain little doubt that he will reach the other side of the Atlantic. At the same time, he confesses that the exact spot on the other side at which he will descend cannot be calculated with any degree of certainty.

TO THE EDITORS OF THE *Express:* It is nearly ten days since the monster balloon began to fill, and people at 25 cents each began to visit it—the receipts being nearly $1,000 per day. Some three days afterwards, when it should have been nearly ready for the ascent, I visited the yard, seeing the top of the balloon above the fence. The gas was shut off because, it was said, the supply was inadequate for the city and couldn't be spared. The papers said the next day it was because the wind was high. It looked to me at the time as though both excuses were a miserable subterfuge; and the taking out of the gas in a large measure since then, when there has not been a decent breeze blowing, has confirmed the impression.

The placards represent a miniature steamboat, with side-wheels, and an engine on board, blowing off steam or smoke. The thing actually there and ready for the ascension is merely a lifeboat of Francis make, with a small windmill shaft thrust out of one end, like a broom handle. The engine was said to be designated to turn this, but a crank a boy can use is substituted.

The placard represents a miniature house, entered with windows on its top, for the daring aeronauts. The reality presents a huge clothesbasket, in which it would be difficult for more than one man to stand erect, to say nothing about sitting down and cooking with the celebrated lime stoves, which are little else than two tin kettles.

If the matter was fairly put before the public, that the proprietor wanted to make money out of people's credulity, very well. But under pretense of a European voyage by which science was to be advanced, and the world astonished, aided by weeks of newspaper heralding in advance—and then to find it little else than *gas*—is rather too much even for New York patience.

Nous Verrons

Without the slightest tremble of motion, we rose gradually higher into the air. Nothing was happening; yet we were inexorably on our way.

It is the unreality that always frightens me the most. I understood why we were moving, and yet my senses failed to back up this understanding. To know that one will travel with the wind, to do so, and then not to feel a whisper of it is disquieting. I agree that the wind and we were as one, but the fact was difficult to reconcile. It was also difficult comprehending the power of the hydrogen gas. I did appreciate how its properties could be put to lifting use in a balloon; but somehow I was unprepared for looking into the gas bag above us, for seeing right inside once the mouth had been opened, and for seeing nothing. It was not there. . . .

The high wind which prevailed early yesterday morning rendered it necessary to discharge the gas from the balloon *City of New York*. The tent, borne down by the force of the wind, fell about 7:30, but no damage was done beyond a temporary suspension of the exhibition. Prof. Lowe, fearing that the balloon would become strained by the action of the wind upon its vast surface, discharged the gas, of which about 65,000 cubic feet had been admitted during the week. The violence of the gale prevented access to the valve rope in the partially filled condition of the envelope, and in order to effect a rapid discharge, one of the seams of the balloon was opened. From this circumstance arose the rumor of an explosion, which was industriously circulated during the day and repeated by the *Evening Post*. The story of a disaster was wholly unfounded. Neither the gas envelope nor the apparatus has sustained any injury. It was originally intended that the exhibition should remain open for a fortnight, and that time having nearly expired, the ascension will probably take place early next week. Should the weather be calm today, Prof. Lowe will make an ascension in his small balloon, *Pioneer,* for the purpose of testing the accuracy of his instruments.

Poised up there, and realizing that all the air above us, below us, and on every side was traveling at our identical speed, I suddenly felt as if in the center of some mighty cohort. It was like being a cavalryman, in the middle of a galloping line. It made me understand what massive forces must be involved when a 20-knot wind moves steadily from one side of a continent to the other. A balloon, unlike any other craft, enables you to feel as part of the elements. A ship is an intrusion, bouncing about on top of the waves; but a balloon is a cloud, a shape on its own, and going with the wind as part of it.

A large crowd was assembled at the Crystal Palace grounds on Saturday to witness an ascension by Prof. Lowe in his balloon, *Pioneer*. The weather was damp and murky, and as the sole object of the contemplated ascension was to test the instruments to be used on the Atlantic trip, the aerial trip of the *Pioneer* was postponed till the first clear day. As it had been announced that the ascension would depend on the state of the weather, no disappointment seemed to be felt by the audience, and the tickets sold for Saturday will be good at another time. The large balloon still lies in a collapsed state.

A new contrivance has been attached to the gas pipe called an "exhauster," by which it is claimed that gas can be passed into the balloon four times faster than the natural pressure would furnish it. It is the intention of Mr. Lowe to commence the inflation of his large balloon the first pleasant day, fill it as speedily as possible, and take his departure for Europe immediately.

The balloonist must realize that a lake passing beneath him will tend to lower his height in the daytime, for the lake will have colder air above it. A wood will have the same effect, and so will marshland, and sea. On the other hand, a town will send him up, just as a hot cornfield will, or a stretch of Tarmac. If the sun emerges from behind a cloud it will cook up his balloon, and send him up higher. When it disappears he will most assuredly come down. In theory, the sun never comes out from the clouds, for both clouds and balloon are moving with the mass of air, but in fact it frequently does, for the airstream is not constant at all heights. It is possible to go faster than the clouds above you. It is more often likely that the clouds will win.

TO THE EDITOR OF THE N.Y. *Express:* Seeing a communication in your paper headed, "Is the Balloon a Humbug?" induces me to say the following few words about Mr. Lowe. He has appropriated to himself the credit of inventions and improvements in balloon making and sailing that justly belong to me, having been published in my book (a copy of which I present to you) issued eight years ago. He also perverts the origin of the idea of a great eastern current in his pamphlet, so as to make it appear that I was not the first to prove that fact. He claims the invention of a sounding line, of a peculiar linseed-oil varnish, of a copper float, of a power in fan wheels to elevate and depress the balloon.

All these things you will find in my book, from which Mr. Lowe has unscrupulously attempted to *pirate* my hard-earned and weatherbeaten thunder in balloon progress to his own glory, or shame, as the case may yet be; and thus I am induced to speak a few words in self-defense.

Mr. Lowe is an aeronaut of 17 months, and of no scientific attainments, and he has not made ten reputable ascensions. By profession he is a "Magician"—by nature a man of very gentlemanly demeanor, by practice in balloon progress an unscrupulous plagiarist.

When Mr. Lowe first disclosed his plan of a big balloon to me in August, he invited me to take a seat in his airship for that voyage; but before he had progressed far in his work, I plainly saw he was deficient in practical knowledge, superficially versed in the philosophy of ballooning; consequently I refused his offer to take passage with him. I refrained from having my name associated with the scheme.

I would only ask, as your correspondent did, why was that most remarkable spell of calm, favorable weather of twelve days just past, not taken advantage of?

If Mr. Lowe has been playing upon public credulity, in order to do something else than try to cross the Atlantic, it should only be considered as one of his biggest "sleight of hand" performances, upon a very big audience, with a very big gas bag made out of nine cents per yard muslin.

As I intend to try the transatlantic voyage myself next summer, you will excuse my being thus plain, as I am also willing to be tried by the same exposure of intentions and abilities that I have candidly awarded Mr. Lowe.

John Wise

So the balloonist flies along, trying to foresee everything, estimating what is likely to send him up or down in five minutes' time, deciding what weight he wants to be then, calculating whether the winds below or above his balloon are moving faster than he is, and keeping stock of a constantly changing situation. It is not easy. If you start rising, for instance, you have to decide whether this move is being caused by the two handfuls of sand thrown out four minutes before, or the sun's becoming slightly brighter, or the farmyard you have just passed over, or if it were none of these three and instead a thermal has taken hold of you . . .

The *Pioneer* was on the spot and inflated to the utmost desirable extent as early as 2:30 P.M. An audience of some 1,600 people assembled to see the first ascent from New York of the daring aeronaut. At 1 o'clock Prof. Lowe appeared on the grounds and assumed direction of all the arrangements. The balloon (which holds about 35,000 cubic feet of gas, and which was made by Prof. Lowe's wife, with a view to making an ascension herself) was brought to the appointed place, and the inflation was commenced. At 2:30 P.M. the globe was filled and the crowd was most uproarious in their demonstrations of delight and impatience. At the last minute, Mr. Lowe's wife, a pleasing-looking, dark-haired, dark-eyed French lady, appeared on the scene, bearing in her arms his child, a boy of about two years old. Mr. Lowe kissed them both fondly, and all having been prepared, he gave the word to start.

The Professor was as cool and self-possessed as if he had been taking his seat in a stagecoach. Just before stepping into the basket, he took off his ordinary overcoat, and put on a bearskin coat and a huge bearskin cap. Then the word was given to let go, the rope was cut, and the balloon rose in nearly a straight line to the height of about two thousand feet, when it began to sail away in a direct easterly course. The last that was seen of him, he was eating an apple and alternately waving his hat and the American flag.

In about ten minutes, another current of air seized the balloon and bore it northeast. When last seen from the Park Observatory at Eighty-sixth street, it appeared to be coming down in the vicinity of White Plains or Tarrytown.

The account of the trip, as given by Mr. Lowe himself, is as follows: he left the Crystal Palace grounds at 3:20 (his watch differed a few minutes from that of our reporter); in five minutes he had attained an altitude of half a mile, whence he had a splendid view of Manhattan Island, Long Island, New Jersey, and in the northern distance, Connecticut. The thermometer, which stood at 65° at starting, fell at this height to 30°. The balloon first took a direction nearly east, when the Professor, finding that a sail in this direction continued for any great length of time would carry him out to sea, applied himself to the valve rope, and discharged a sufficient quantity of gas to bring him down into an undercurrent of air running in a direction nearly northeast. He kept the *Pioneer* in this favorable gale until he had been borne inland so far that no more danger was to be apprehended from the water, when he resolved to return to earth again. The discharge of a few cubic feet of gas was sufficient to effect this.

At least 500 persons assembled on the spot where the balloon just touched the earth, and Mr. Lowe was welcomed with huge quantities of cheering. The crowd was most enthusiastic, so much so that the accommodating Professor, willing to gratify their innocent and laudable curiosity, resolved to make a second ascension for their especial benefit. Accordingly, having drunk a bottle of ale to the health of the assembled multitude, he hove out about ten or twenty pounds of sand, and away he went again. On the second ascension he had reached a height of one mile. He was saluted by the whistles of multitudinous steamboats and of several railway trains. Remaining in the air about twenty minutes, he descended on the farm of Mr. G. W. Busteed, having achieved the distance of twelve miles. On reaching the ground he handed Mr. Busteed a copy of one of the New York evening papers, which had left New York an hour before.

The aeronaut discharged the gas from the *Pioneer*, rolled her into a compact ball, put her into a wagon, and started for New York, reaching the city at 7:15. Mr. Lowe first saw his wife, to assure her of his safety, and then proceeded to the Everett House to meet a party to celebrate his safe return in divers performances, which were not concluded till this morning.

We understand that the Professor intends to start on his transatlantic trip in the great balloon, the *City of New York,* on Saturday next.

A man who has taken some tasteless poison, the effects of which will not be apparent for awhile, must consider his situation as curiously unreal. On the one hand he feels perfectly fit, and on the other he knows that he will soon be disastrously ill. So, for that fatal interregnum, he stands there, feeling perfectly well in body, and wondering what will happen next.

To a certain degree we felt like that man. There was nothing wrong with us, save that we were in a basket poised momentarily well over a mile above the ground, depending upon a few ropes and a bag of gas.

An accident happened to Prof. Lowe's balloon last night during a blow. The huge globe of the balloon was lifted with a jerk, dragging for several feet the heavy sandbags that served as weights to keep it down, causing them to dance around like puppet dolls. A few rods to the east of the balloon stands a small hut containing rope and other articles in constant use. Against the sharp ridge pole of this tent the balloon was blown with great violence, breaking a hole in the muslin through which the gas rushed in dense volumes. In a few moments the 68,000 feet of gas in the balloon had escaped, and the lately expanded globe presented the appearance of a collapsed mass of flabby rag, involving the proprietor in a dead loss of nearly $3,000. It will be repaired immediately and the inflation resumed.

At five o'clock, thunder-gusts were approaching the track of our balloon. We were low enough now to hear the wind rustling in the trees. A great many persons following the balloon. Some gave up the chase; others struck in with fresh vigor. Vivid flashes of lightning were occasionally seen in the north. Here I ceased taking notes—the car was near the treetops—thick woods underneath, and a roaring thunderstorm just ahead. . . .

Prof. Lowe's
MAMMOTH AERIAL SHIP
CITY OF NEW YORK
Is Now Nearly Inflated
For Its
Grand Transatlantic Voyage
THE ASCENSION
WILL POSITIVELY TAKE PLACE
TODAY (SATURDAY) 19 INSTANT
AT 12 O'CLOCK, NOON
IF THE WEATHER IS CALM;
IF NOT, ON THE FIRST CALM DAY FOLLOWING.
(SUNDAY EXCEPTED)
Tickets (for this day only) 25 cents
Tickets on day of Ascension 50 cents

TO THE EDITOR OF THE NEW YORK *Tribune: Sir:* In announcing a postponement, I feel that some explanation is due to the public for the apparent delay which has occurred in connection with my proposed aerial voyage to Europe. The whole matter may be stated in a few words.

234

To inflate so large a vehicle as the *City of New York* requires (considering the facilities afforded by the gas company) at least sixty hours of reasonably fair weather and a continuous flow of gas. Every preparation had been made to start today. The present stormy weather has not only interfered with the inflation, which began yesterday at 3 o'clock, but continues to retard our operations to such an extent as to make it somewhat problematical to fix the precise day of departure.

The public may rest assured that the earliest practicable moment will be made available for the object I have in view, and that no effort will be foregone that may insure the success of this, the first voyage upon the "wings of the wind" from the new to the old world.

While the project is grand, magnificent, and beautiful to contemplate, the public should not forget that it is nonetheless laborious, expensive, and hazardous; and should I succeed in the attempt, those who now hesitate to give me their confidence may awake to the fact that "in the bright lexicon of youth, there is no such word as fail." Had my operations been conducted immediately near the works of the gas company, the inflation might have been accomplished in ten hours or less.

Should I, Mr. Editor, be the humble means of advancing the interests of science, and in some measure adding to the glory of our common country, I shall be more than repaid for the long months of thought, and research, and labor, that I have contributed to the accomplishment of the great design I have in view.

Believing in the kind indulgence of a liberal public, I am,

T. S. C. Lowe

Crystal Palace Grounds, Nov. 16—
6 P.M. We yesterday saw the great
balloon. It was said to be only one-
third inflated; yet the top was almost
level with the parapet of the reservoir. The wind was blowing heavily,
and the huge gas bag was only kept
from being driven off into the air by
several hundred sacks of sand, in
the aggregate about 25 tons, which
anchored it to the earth. As it was,
the machine was in great danger of
bursting from the violence of the
storm. Mr. Lowe says that a new
obstacle to his departure has arisen.
His marine navigator has fallen dangerously ill and cannot go. He
therefore desires us to state that he
will be happy to effect an engagement with any competent mariner
who may wish to go with him.

*The landing, defined by others as a controlled accident at the
best of times, is always a remarkable occurrence.*

*We choose our field and unfasten the trail rope. We shout at
people, if people there be, to catch hold of it. We throw out sand
to lessen the fall, if it grows too severe. We start overrunning the
field, so we valve again to get down more rapidly. We go too fast.
More sand.*

*A man catches hold of the rope. It pulls him off his feet. We
shout at him, then see a wire fence approaching and shout
harder. His friend catches hold, we valve, and search for more
sand. . . .*

CITY ITEMS

JONATHAN TO LOWE

by Jacques Maurice

I've seen your Gas Bag, Mister Lowe,
And paid a quarter for the show.
I haven't had so grand a treat
Since Blondin come his circus-feat.

But when will you inflatuate?
The season, Lowe, is getting late—
You said you would, some time ago,
Yet you continue for to show!

You stay and stay, and feather your nest,
While Vic., and Nap., and all the rest,
Are waiting for your flying visit;
It ain't a dodge, nor nothin', is it?

I've heard it whispered, Mister Lowe—
I re'ly hope it isn't so—
I'm sure I don't pretend to know:
They say—you never meant to go.

A man is lucky that's got brass—
A man is lucky that's got gas;
With brass and gas, and backers, too,
A smart man ought to wiggle through!

The ground comes up fast. We hit it and fall into the bottom of the basket. We pick ourselves up and look for the valve line. We strike again. The basket then strikes the fence. There is a rushing sound of wind. The basket is dragging over the field.

You can't find anything, but you must rip. You must get rid of the gas. The poplars are coming close. You look for the red rope. *You pull it. You take up its slack, lose it, then pull again, and this time you can feel it jerking open the panel. The balloon above you flaps wildly once or twice, and then lies down, softly, gracefully, on the bit of field in front of you. . . .*

The balloon exhibition of Prof. Lowe is finally closed for the season, and the promised aerial trip to Europe postponed—mainly "on account of the weather." All the apparatus having been removed from the Palace grounds, visitors who were allured to the spot on Thursday to witness an ascension in the small balloon, found the great globe gone. The heavy blow on Thanksgiving Day rendered the preliminary ascension impossible, so that no visitors were admitted and no money received. The balloon has been carried to a place near the gashouse at the foot of Fourteenth street, North River, where it will remain until spring.

If all goes well, the fabric of the balloon will then remain manageable on the ground, rolling as the wind blows and ruckles its surfaces, the balloonists snarled in a ridiculous medley of legs, arms, sandbags, instruments, water bottles, and much else besides; lying there laughing, and asking each other if they are all right.

238

Planting one's feet upon the ground once more—still glowing from the flight—all will discover that at that moment in time, one is a king.